Primrose Hill Manor

The history of the Janetville mansion

BANNISTER PRESS

Contents

Dear Reader   1

Foreword   3
by Emily Turner, PhD

First Nations   5

Janet   7

Lot Six in the Thirteenth Concession   9
an overview of the property, dwellings, and owners

Primrose Hill Manor   23

Christmas at the Manor   76

The Allan family   83
lived in the house 1885 - 1892

The Nasmyth family   95
lived in the house 1892 - 1906

The McCulloch family   107
lived in the house 1906 - 190

The Johnston family   110
lived in the house 1908 - 1918

The Porter family   114
lived in the house 1918 - 1962

The Davis family   119
lived in the house 1962 - 1966

The Gentile family   127
lived in the house 1966 - 1970

The Gordon family   131
lived in the house 1970 - 2021

The Sopoci family   135
lived in the house 2021 - 2024

Sources   139

Photography Credits   151

Acknowledgements   152

Dear Reader,

I am delighted to present to you this beautiful book, a labour of love dedicated to a true gem of our community—the 1885 Italianate Victorian home that I had the honour of calling my own for three wonderful years. It is a house that has not only stood the test of time but has also become a beloved landmark, cherished by all who have had the pleasure of witnessing her grandeur.

My hope for author Sara Walker-Howe in taking on this project was born out of a desire to share the rich history and architectural beauty of this remarkable home with a wider audience. It is a house that has seen the ebb and flow of generations, stood as a testament to the craftsmanship of a bygone era, and held within its walls countless stories and memories. As you turn these pages, you will be transported back in time, discovering the unique features and intricate details that make this house a true treasure.

I envisioned this book as more than just a chronicle of a house; I saw it as a bridge connecting the past to the present, allowing readers to appreciate the historical significance and timeless beauty of this architectural masterpiece. From its role as a doctor's house to its preservation of original features, this home embodies a legacy that is meant to be shared with the world. And I am forever grateful for Sara in bringing this book to life.

It is my hope that through this book, you will come to appreciate the charm and character of this splendid Victorian home as much as I have. May it inspire you, as it has inspired me, to cherish and preserve the architectural heritage that enriches our communities.

Paulette Sopoci

Foreword

BY EMILY TURNER, PhD

The Janetville Mansion is an architectural treasure in Kawartha Lakes. Known locally as the Doctor's House, it is one of the most distinctive historic homes in Manvers Township and, indeed, in the wider Kawartha Lakes area. Built in 1885 by local doctor William Allan to an ornate and ambitious Italianate design, this house was designated under the Ontario Heritage Act in 2010 to preserve and celebrate its superb architectural features and importance to the hamlet of Janetville as a well-loved local landmark. The Italianate home has been recently and lovingly restored and preserved to its late nineteenth century glory and is a model of both the architectural ambitions of the mid-1880s and of sensitive heritage conservation in the present. Its stunning and intricate architectural details have been conserved and made to shine, while firmly creating an inviting space for modern-day living.

However, a house is more than its technical and architectural features. This book traces the history of the house, its owners, and their role in the evolution of Janetville. The occupants of this house are brought to life through detailed historic research, tracing their time in Janetville and beyond, reminding us that their stories make the house a living, breathing piece of our collective history and memory.

Heritage is about buildings but it is also about people and this book celebrates both, anchoring a spectacular piece of Italianate architecture in place, time and the lives lived within it. Our understanding of heritage and what it means to our communities has evolved substantially since the first buildings in Ontario were designated under the newly created Ontario Heritage Act in 1975. Although then, as now, we understand the importance of heritage features and attributes – the grand Italianate façade, the sweeping Jacobean staircase, the delicate moulding and ceiling medallions – to the physical presence of a historic building, its history and its people truly define it in its community.

Through this book, you are invited to explore a fascinating piece of Janetville's history through a beautiful historic house and the families who called it home. Learn about its stories, enjoy its gorgeous architecture, and be inspired to explore and understand the incredible heritage buildings, both plain and ornate, around you and the people who created them.

Emily Turner is the Economic Development Officer – Heritage Planning for the City of Kawartha Lakes. She holds a Doctor of Philosophy degree in Architecture from the University of Edinburgh.

First Nations

The land discussed in this book spans the traditional territory of the Anishinabewaki ⊲σ∫·ὰ V·⊲P, Wen-dake-Nionwentsïo, Ho-de-no-sau-nee-ga (Haudenosaunee), Mississauga peoples, part of Treaty 20, 1818.

Nionwentsïo, from the Wendat language, means "Our magnificent territory."

Haudenosaunee means "People of the Longhouse."

Anishinaabe translates to "People from whence lowered." The Anishinaabe believed that their people were created by divine breath.

Although this book is about post-colonial times and people, please remember those who cared for the land before the colonists. The people of this magnificent territory, builders of longhouses, each of us existing for the duration of an exhale of a god.

After Paulette Sopoci moved into the Janetville mansion, a neighbour told her of a time in the settler days when there was a cupboard near her house that was shared with the First Nations peoples. It was an outdoor icebox where settlers put jars of jam and returned later to find the jam was gone, but in its place they would find fresh trapped meat.

Through exchanges like these, the settlers survived harsh winters and the hardships of establishing the land for farming.

Janet

It's long been claimed that the village of Janetville was named for Janet McDermid, wife of the owner of McDermid Saw Mills and first postmaster for the village, (though some sources say she was his daughter.) And some claim this story is not true at all, that Janet—if she existed—certainly was not the first postmaster since official records do not name her as such.

According to the official records held by Library and Archives of Canada, the first postmaster was John McDermid. He was appointed on 1 November 1862 and vacated his post when he moved away in 1870. Reported on the 1861 Census, there was a John McDermid in the area, 31 years old, working as a miller, and married to Janet McDermid, also 31 years old. They lived in a log cabin that was built in 1857. From this we can see that Janet did exist and was the wife of the official postmaster on record.

It's interesting to note that on the 1861 Census, McDermid's name is spelled "Jennet" and in 1871 her name is spelled "Gannet." This is of particular interest because the village was spelled "Genetsville" in the Illustrated Historical Atlas of the counties of Northumberland and Durham, Ont., published in 1878, which further strengthens the tie between McDermid and the name of the village. This may be a spelling error, though, since prior to 1878, newspapers referred to the village as "Janetville" but the coincidence of spelling in the census and atlas shouldn't be wholly discounted.

Given that her husband is listed as the postmaster, it seems likely that "Janetville" was indeed named for Janet McDermid, wife of John McDermid. And given that her husband was a miller in 1861 and farmer in 1871, it also seems likely that she may have covered the postmaster duties for her husband. Officially, women weren't allowed to be postmasters. In fact, a widow was fired from her postmaster duties in Coboconk in 1891. The first published reference of Janet McDermid as the first postmaster was in the Lindsay Post in 1952, and seems highly probable that at the time of the article there would have been a few people around who remembered stories of the early days of Janetville, including Janet McDermid as first postmaster— whatever official documents might say.

Janet was born to Peter Christie and Christina MacDermid on November 5, 1829 in Cornwall, Ontario. She married John McDermid and moved to Manvers township with her husband and his brother, Neil. The brothers started a mill on a pond and the village grew up around the area. Prior to this, there were a few farmers in the area, but no village.

Janet and John had three children: Margaret, Peter and Duncan. When John died in 1890, Janet moved to Lindsay to live with her daughter. Janet died on July 5, 1919 and was buried at Riverside Cemetery in Lindsay.

Janet's brother-in-law, Neil, married Margaret McKinnon and moved to Port Perry. They later relocated to the London area of Ontario, where two of his sons started the O-Pee-Chee Gum Company in 1911.

On that same pond, known as Mill Pond, John Burn and Henry Irwin started a mill in 1800, and in 1854, John Burn started a general store. After the McDermids moved out of the area, the post office was located in the Burns' general store. The store has continued operation through each generation and is still going strong today.

While researching this book, it became apparent that a number of Janets were connected to the Janetville mansion:
Janet Edward Bonnar (mother of Dr. William Allan, 1st owner of the house)
Janet Wylie (mother of Jane Primrose Morrison Nasmyth, 2nd owner of the house)
Janet Wylie Nasmyth (daughter of Jane Primrose Morrison Nasmyth)
Janet Forrester Morrison (mother of David Morrison, Jane Primrose Nasmyth's father)

Photo from the Burn family collection of Janetville folks on a cart in front of the mansion. Probably 1920s.

Lot Six in the Thirteenth Concession

AN OVERVIEW OF THE PROPERTY, DWELLINGS, AND OWNERS

The original lot consisted of 200 acres, and in 1817, the Crown granted this parcel to Duncan McDonnell, a surveyor who mapped out the lots and concessions of the area, like he did for much of central Ontario. As part of his wages, he was given acreage wherever he worked, including this lot, but he didn't live here. He lived in Greenfield, Glengarry County, in the far eastern corner of Ontario near Ottawa and Cornwall, though he owned lots in virtually every county he surveyed.

In 1831, lot 6 concession 13 ended up in the hands of Henry Ruttan, the sheriff for Newcastle District. (Before this municipality was Kawartha Lakes, it was Victoria County. Before that it was conjoined with Peterborough County, and before that, the twin counties were grouped within Newcastle District, formed in 1802, when it splintered from the much larger Home District.) On March 9, the sheriff took possession of the land by way of a sheriff's deed. We don't know exactly why the land was taken by the law. Perhaps McDonnell didn't pay the taxes on the land. Perhaps McDonnell directed the sheriff to sell it; he certainly had more land than he could use. In any case, the land was in the hands of Sheriff Ruttan, a Cobourg resident, for two years.

On January 25, 1833, the 200 acres were purchased by Ephraim Powell for a whole £4. Two days later, he sold the property to Robert McGill for £72, pocketing an incredible profit for the time. It seems likely Powell bought the land at a sheriff's auction, recognizing an opportunity. At the time, Ontario had begun to flood the land with immigrants, many of them farmers, and Powell, who lived in Cobourg, was correctly positioned to find a buyer from the many new citizens passing through the area on their way to new lands.

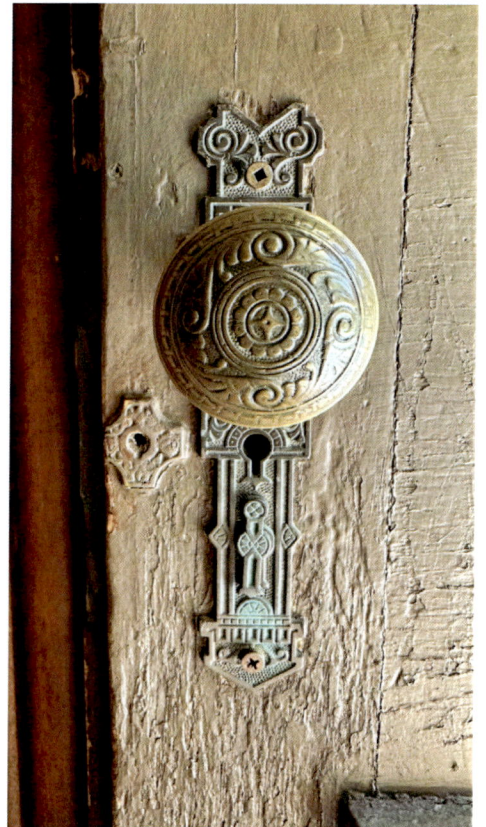

Robert McGill also recognized an opportunity. After making his purchase, a day later, he severed 100 acres from the north half and sold them to John McGill for half of what he'd paid. We know John McGill possibly lived somewhere on the 100 acres, in a log house while he farmed on the property. The McGill name is still in the area.

In 1851, John McGill sold his 100 acres to Samuel McGee for £175. Likely by this time, the land was cleared and ready for farming and possibly even contained a dwelling, but such a log house was not likely on the five acres that became Primrose Hill Manor.

The First Dwellings

In 1864, for unknown reasons, Samuel McGee severed off five acres and sold them to Henry Gillespie, a carpenter. Gillespie had been living nearby in the home of Wesly Defoe, a carriage maker. Recently married and with an infant daughter and another child on the way, Gillespie purchased the five acres, so it seems likely he may have built a house. At the time, houses were mainly of log or frame construction.

When Gillespie died in July 1868, his will instructed the land to go back to Robert McGill. That transaction was registered at the same time as the sale of the 5 acres by Annie J. Gillespie et al to Thomas Timmins in May 1871 for $1405. The Census of 1871 shows Anne Jane Gillespie living in Janetville with her children Margaret Sophia, Robert Henry and Minnie, where all but Minnie are listed by their middle names. This appears to be a quirk of the census taker; anyone with a middle name is listed by first name initial and full middle name. Despite the oddity, the census shows the family living together, which indicates they were in their own dwelling. Unfortunately, more information about the dwelling was not part of this census.

The barn at Primrose Hill Manor.

The family listed after the Gillespies on the 1871 Census is Thomas Timmins, his wife Martha, and their four children. This likely makes Timmins family the next-door neighbours to the Gillespies just five years prior to Thomas Timmins purchasing the five acres that would more than a hundred years later become known as Primrose Hill Manor. The Timmins took out a couple of mortgages against the property: $1000 with George Lumsden (a Scottish labourer who lived in Newcastle) and $438 with John McDonald.

The Timmins family operated the first store in Janetville. Thomas and Robert opened the store in Janetville in 1854. According to a 1952 article in the Post, "the Timmins family bought the property which is now owned by Mrs. James Porter and lived retired." (The Porters would be the fifth family to own Primrose Hill Manor.)

For whatever reason, the deed was in George Lumsden's hands when he sold to John McAlpine in September 1879 for $600, possibly the balance of the mortgage owed, as the deed seems to have reverted back to Lumsden, cutting out the Timmins.

Door bell pull (left) outside the front door rings the bell (right) in the main hall.

However it happened, this transaction put the property in the hands of a doctor. It was widely thought that McAlpine was Janetville's first doctor, since he began his practice there in 1884, but he was actually the village's second doctor. The honour of being first goes to Hugh Richard McGill, born in Manvers township in 1861. He passed his entrance exams before the College of Physicians and Surgeons in 1877 and passed his final exams in 1882. His address was listed in the publication, *Announcement of the College of Physicians and Surgeons*, as Janetville. McAlpine arrived in 1884 when McGill moved to Medonte in Simcoe County.

McAlpine did not live in the Doctor's House, though it has been widely thought he did. In 1992, Wallace McAlpine, Eliza's grandson, cleared the matter up entirely in a letter, "When I said to Eliza people were saying that Dr. John had lived in the big mansion in Janetville, her reply was: 'Oh, gracious, no! We were too poor. We had nothing whatever to do with it.' This was confirmed by my father Bernie." In fact, Eliza said Dr. John was often paid in barter. "A payment might be a bushel of oats or a bag of potatoes. For one operation he received a goose." Doesn't sound like he had the means to construct the large Italianate home. Did he have the means to own multiple properties? Possibly. Land was cheap at the time, and it's possible he accepted portions of land as payment, so perhaps that is how he arrived at owning these five acres, but it's also possible the McAlpines lived on this parcel of land.

According to the memoirs of Eliza Hughes McAlpine, recorded by her grandson Wallace McAlpine, "John's home and office was a log house, up a long lane, on the east side of the road, opposite Burn's General Store. There was a small log barn where his horse was stabled." (McAlpine, page 32)

If Eliza's memory is correct, this puts the McAlpines in the *south half* of lot six. It's possible they *lived* in the south half and *owned* the five acres in the north half. But it's also possible that if they were as poor as Eliza said, they might not have owned multiple properties, and given that during Eliza's time in Janetville there were stores located across the road from the mansion property, it's possible the memories are not quite correct and the McAlpines did live on the mansion property.

The trouble is, Wallace wrote the memoirs fifty years after Eliza's death, in the 1980s. He was thirteen in 1927 when went to live with Eliza and began asking her about the early days. When writing the memoir, he was drawing from his own memories of these discussions with Eliza and not all of his facts were correct. Resources for fact-checking were not as vastly available as they are today.

For example, Wallace says that during the time when the McAlpines were living in Janetville, "Dr. Robert Allen [sic] was already established in the area. To the north of the village, he was building one of the most beautiful and elegant mansions to be seen in Ontario." (McAlpine, page 32) We know now that it was Dr. William Allan who built the mansion, and with some research into the Allan family, we also know he was not in Ontario at the same time the McAlpines were in Janetville. The 1881 Scotland Census shows Dr. Allan, fresh out of medical school, was living with his uncle in Scotland.

We know from the land registry records that the McAlpines owned the property until December 1884 when they moved to Lindsay and sold the property to Dr. William Allan for $4000– a big jump from the $600 they paid for the property. The jump in price here would certainly indicate the construction or upgrade of a dwelling during the McAlpines' time. The memoir says the McAlpines started out in a log cabin, but doesn't mention if they upgraded their living situation during their time in Janetville, and five years is certainly long enough to construct a house. The McAlpines could have built a frame house and added or upgraded a barn.

It's unfortunate we can't count on Wallace's memoir as fact because the memoir could have provided some wonderful local history. As Wallace says, "It never occurred to me to make notes of her wonderful stories. Never have I regretted this omission more." (McAlpine, page 89)

Although the house wasn't built by Dr. McAlpine, we do know the house was built by a doctor. In 1885, Dr. William Allan built the Janetville mansion. And a second house on the property: an Ontario Gothic Cottage.

The Ontario Gothic Cottage in Lotus.

The Ontario Gothic Cottage was removed from the property and relocated 13 km south of Janetville in Lotus. Though there's no official document to support this, the house was moved by the Nasmyth family for youngest son, James Nasmyth, since he's shown on the land registry as owning the part lot in Lotus from 1897 to 1899, where the house is now located, and he'd freshly married Emma Armstrong in 1896. He bought the land for $100 and sold for $650; likely making a nice profit because the house was added to the land. His older brother, John, was already in Lotus, operating a general store, and had been established there for many years.

When she was interviewed in 1980, John Nasmyth's daughter, Myrtle McTear, confirmed the Nasmyth family moved the house to Lotus. "At one time a second house stood on the property to the north of the mansion. This house was utilized as the servants quarters and laundry. The brick building was torn down and moved to Lotus in the time of the Naismiths.[sic]" (Post 1980) The Nasmyth family had the knowledge and means to move the house, as well, due to Jane Primrose's husband John being a contractor who cleared land and built railroads.

The dwelling is a perfect example of an Ontario Gothic cottage in yellow brick, though simple and economic in design. It stands at one and half stories, with windows slightly rounded at the top, and without ornate features. There's no porch or bargeboard and only a simple transom window above the door. The Ontario Gothic cottages became quite popular after 1864.

The yellow cottage bears a number of similarities to the villa mansion: the same yellow brick and the similar shape of the windows with the eyebrow brick-trim above the windows. Myrtle McTear said that when the cottage was on the land in Janetville, it was used as a washing house and servant's quarters.

Donald Sutcliffe's great-grandmother, a member of the local Magill family, was a young girl when the house was moved. The great event was one she remembered for the rest of her life. She recalled a long parade of horse-drawn carts carrying away loads of bricks and materials. What a site that would have been!

The exact origins of the first dwellings on the property may be uncertain, but we now know that the yellow buff Italianate that became known as the Doctor's House was in fact constructed by Dr. William Allan.

The Doctor's House

The Heritage Designation states the house was built in 1880. This is because of an assumption made by Jack Gordon, the 8th owner of the house. In an interview in 1980, he said, "Why do I think the home was erected in 1880, why because of the date shown on the metal radiator covers." This assumption also fed into the idea that Dr. McAlpine built the house. While these assumptions are not correct, they were good guesses for the information that was available at the time.

Maker stamp reads: W. King March 1880

In 1885, the Warder wrote, "Dr. Allan is about beginning operations on his new mansion. He made a bee one day last week, and 44 teams responded to the call. A large number of bricks were laid on the ground but not enough to do. All could not attend, but they will when the hurry is over. We hear he is going to raise a very commodious building. We congratulate him on his enterprise." In 1906, the Lindsay Post wrote about various doctors shifting to new locations, including the "fine residence, 'Manverston Hall', built by Dr. Wm. Allan, recently of Lindsay at a cost of $12,000."

Further, in the obituary for Kate Porter, owner of the house with her husband John James Porter from 1918 to 1962, the Lindsay Post stated, "Mrs. Porter lived in the 'Doctor's House'-- the imposing large residence built by Doctor Allan and purchased by Mr. Porter after his retirement from the farm." (Post 1964)

It was also widely thought that the house was built by William's brother, Dr. Robert Allan, as stated by Eliza McAlpine and by Violet Carr in *The Rolling Hills*, but this could not be possible because until 1886, Robert was in medical school in Scotland.

The house was undoubtedly built by Dr. William Allan in 1885.

Dr. Allan constructed the big Italianate house in a big way, paying tribute to his Scottish roots in many details throughout the house, from the Jacobean staircase to the ruby flash glass with Celtic etchings. Kate Porter's obituary mentions the house was constructed "of imported materials of stone and woodwork from overseas." (Post 1964)

Then, in 1892, when Dr. Allan left Janetville to practise in Lindsay, he sold the property with the two houses to Jane Primrose Nasmyth, wife of John Nasmyth. (Incidentally, both Dr. Allan and Jane Primrose had mothers named Janet.) The Nasmyths were only in the house for three years when Jane Primrose died. In her will, she left the house to her children, who sold the house to John Nasmyth, (her husband and their father) for $1. Two years later, John sold the house to their son, Dr. William Wylie Nasmyth for $6000. Dr. Nasmyth acquired and paid off several mortgages during his time as the homeowner, likely making upgrades and changes to the property, or perhaps to add livestock to his horse breeding business. The Nasmyths continued the name "Manverston Hall" for the house, and in 1906, Nasmyth moved to Lindsay to practise, selling to Dr. John McCulloch.

At the time, Dr. McCulloch was practising in Lindsay, and at the urging of his patients, he made the trek to Lindsay once a week to see patients. This only lasted for a year and half before he moved to Lindsay again, taking up residence in the former home of Dr. Herriman on Cambridge Street. He sold the Janetville mansion to Dr. James Linton Johnston for $4000.

Dr. Johnston only practised until 1911, when he died of a sudden brain tumour. His wife Kate Sara (McLeod) and daughter, Martha Linton Johnston, continued to live in the house until 1918, when they sold it to John James Porter for a loss at $2900. Dr. Johnston's death ended the reign of physicians in the Doctor's House.

Post-Doctor Era

John Porter, a farmer, lived in the house until his death in 1941. His wife, known locally to everyone as "Aunt Kate", continued to live there until two years before her death in 1964. For $5000, she sold it to William Carl Irwin Davis, an employee of General Motors.

Just five years later, Bill Davis sold the house to Crescenzo and Sylvia Gentile. Jack Gordon credited the Gentiles for their timely purchase, saying they were "the right purchaser at the right time and spent much time and money in restoring the house." The Gentiles sold to Mr. Gordon on 31 August 1970. During Jack's time, the house was known as "Manvers Hall" and "the Casa Loma of Janetville" and "the Doctor's House."

Jack Gordon did not move into the house immediately. From 1970 to 1972, he rented the house to the Kapitan family. Mark Kapitan was five years old when they moved in; his brothers were three and one. His father worked at John Deyell Printing in Lindsay.

When the municipality renamed the roads, the property came to be known as 746 Janetville Road. Mr. Gordon was the person to occupy the house for the longest, until he reluctantly sold it to Paulette Sopoci in 2021.

Heritage plaque outside the main entrance.

The house received its Heritage Designation in June 2010. Attributes conserved included:
- buff brickwork, original windows and shutters, two sets of double front doors with etched glass

- Exterior 4-pane and double-hung windows

- Two-storey Italianate verandas, which includes a polaza (Italianate) on the ground floor terrace and a balcony with French doors on the first and second floors

- Inlaid parquet floorings in the main entrance

- Two fireplaces on the second floor — 1) original Eastlake fireplace in the library, 2) fireplace in the master bedroom with Gothic style mantel

- Vaulted ceiling in the second floor library

- One main Jacobean staircase in the foyer leading to the second floor

- Decorative balustrade across the top of landing

Paulette named the house "Primrose Hill Manor" before she'd researched the home's history, so she was surprised when she learned Jane Primrose Nasmyth was one of the previous owners of the house.

The various wallpapers in the house in 2021.

Primrose Hill Manor

The structure of Primrose Hill Manor is primarily Italianate in the "villa" style. Characteristics of the Italianate style include structural elements as the cubic form, the low-pitched hip roof, the cupola or Italian belvedere atop the house, and the single-story wraparound porch. This style also includes decorative elements such as the quoins (the alternating brickwork at the building's corners), the window hoods (sometimes called eyebrows) and the large-scrolled ornamental brackets under the deeply projecting eaves.

"At one point (probably when the house was built) there was a widow's walk (sometimes referred to as a widow's watch) on the roof. It was removed for whatever reasons but the foundation was left in place. Just recently I contacted Travis Windsor to build a new widow's walk on part of the original foundation, using windows stored either in the barn or in the attic. There are 12 windows: 4 on either side and 2 on either end. The walk was completed on Monday, June 22, 2015. The restoration is now finished to my complete satisfaction." (Jack Gordon, 2015)

Plans for a similar design appeared in volume 2, issue 8 of The Canada Farmer on April 15, 1865, where the style was simply titled "a two-story farm-house." This design is also cubic in form with quoins and the same pattern of window hoods. The farm-house plans included a two-foot front projection at the front of the house. This same projection can be seen in Primrose Hill Manor, although clearly, the second-floor porch was incorporated into the Manor's design.

At the time of the Manor's construction, the Queen Anne Revival had begun, and the Victorian craftsmanship can be seen in the details of the front projection. The diagonal inlaid siding is also reminiscent of the stick or Eastlake style of decorative woodwork.

Local bricks were made of the iron-rich red clay, manufactured in the area along the Scugog River just south of Lindsay by the Fox and Curtain families. It's likely the buff bricks used to construct the Manor and the cottage were from the Don Valley Brick Works, Toronto, which was the largest maker of buff-clay bricks at the time. In 1891, the yard produced as many as 44,000 bricks per day. The cost to deliver by wagon would have been high, which is likely why the buff bricks are often incorporated only in details, such as quoining or window hoods, in other houses in Kawartha Lakes.

GARDEN AND GROUNDS

When Jack Gordon moved into the house in 1972, he made the landscaping one of his first priorities. He said, "The grounds had been left unattended and looked like wilderness." Extensive brush had to be removed and parts of the land re-levelled. He added a swimming pool to the east of the house for his nieces, and a pond to the front.

> "A cast iron fence along the front of my property facing the road will be started this week. The contractor is McFaul Fencing Ltd on Cigar Road, Courtice, Ontario...Construction fully completed on July 23, 2015." (Jack Gordon, 2015)

Jack Gordon added many garden statues throughout the property. Some pieces are replicas of well-known works, including the Venus de Milo and the statue of David by Michelangelo.

He added a pond to the front of the house and the iron fence. Although the pond was filled in, the fence and statues remain, now surrounded by beautiful flower gardens.

Entrance and Main Hallway

The entrance doors and transom light are adorned with ruby flash glass with celtic etchings, harkening back to William Allan's Scottish roots. The glass gets its colour from a coating of copper sulphide solution and being baked in a kiln. The patterns are then etched into the red coating.

Inside the entrance is the breathtaking formal centre hall. From the inlaid pattern on the floor, to the grand staircase and the chandelier high above, gorgeous detail abound.

The staircase is said to be made of imported rosewood with the railing and spindles of walnut. The design is said to be Jacobean or inspired by the asthetic movement.

Semi-floating, the staircase also sports an engaged newell post with a drop finial.

Playing peek-a-boo is Sherlock, Paulette's sister's dog.

Front Parlour

With the large bay window, the front parlour was rarely used by the family during the Nasmyths' time. This area was likely the doctor's examining room, since it provided the most light with its tall windows and southern exposure. During the Porter's time, Aunt Kate rented out this space to a hairdresser.

"As I recall one of the walls was covered in velvet with patterns on it." (Mrs. McTear, Post 1980)

The mirror above the fireplace is from London, England. Note the Wedgwood insert. The chandelier in this room is from Paris.

The front parlour contains a mystery door that does not fully open. It is narrower than a normal door and slides open from the bottom, like a window, but only opens a few feet. One theory suggests the door is meant to allow airflow, but it would seem if that were the case, a window would have been more practical. A more gruesome theory names this the death door, used to transport the dead when the front parlour needed to host a funeral. While this could be a Victorian superstition that prevented the living and the dead from sharing an entrance and exit, the frame is too narrow to pass a coffin through. A stretcher could possibly fit.

A happier theory suggest this may have been a door for pets of the household, allowing cats and dogs to enter and exit on their own. This theory is nice, but you wouldn't want muddy paws on the carpets.

The mystery remains.

Rear Parlour

The front parlour and rear parlour are separated by an archway with double corbels that were lovingly restored during the Manor's recent renovations.

Although this rear parlour became a dining room for the post-doctor families, this area was likely the doctor's office space with the desk before the fireplace. With a separate entrance from the south porch, this could have been the place where the doctor could interview their patients or discuss settling a bill.

Dining Parlour

The original dining room was to the east of the main hall and next to kitchen. Dr. Nasmyth used this room as a waiting room for his patients.

The panelling in the room was added by Enzo Gentile. A narrow door once led to the yard, but since has been adapted into a window.

The room is now used as a family room.

The kitchen is the one room that has undergone the most transformations over the years. When the house was originally constructed, the cooking was done in the 'summer kitchen' that was attached to the north side of the house, through this kitchen door. This room also had an outhouse that was used in the winter.

Since the summer kitchen has been removed, this door opens to the pool yard.

Second Floor

The second floor boasts the original railing, installed at a lower height than is required by today's standards. It is protected from change under the heritage designation. The decorative, double-arched balustrade is also protected.

The English chandelier is over 480 years old and features candles for lighting. These days the candles are battery-operated.

The second floor contains a grand open hall that served as a private parlour for the family during the early years. When the doctor was receiving patients in the main floor double parlour and the dining parlour was used as a waiting room, the family retreated to the second floor.

"At the south end of the upper hall, in the days gone-by, stood a grand piano that, according to Mrs. McTear, was played by her grandmother [Jane Primrose Nasmyth]. "My great grandfather, David Morrison, played a Stradivarius," she commented." (Post 1980)

"The room, just beyond the piano area, was used as a room for the keeping of flowers, and three canaries. "Aunt Nellie [Helen Nasmyth] loved flowers," said Mrs. McTear." (Post 1980)

"According to Mrs. McTear, one of the rooms was furnished with single beds for four children. At the yule season of the year a Christmas tree would help create a fairyland to the delight of the children, this room also has a fireplace." (Post 1980) Now the master bedroom.

Library

"My favourite room in the whole place was the library. I remember the wonderful smell in the library. The shelves were lined with red leather, all books looked the same, red leather binding, someone had been proud and particular about what was put on those shelves" - Doris Quibell

The second-floor library "had the most beautiful blue and white tile around the fireplace. I recall hearing the tile was imported from Spain." - Doris Quibell

Attic

A narrow staircase winds from the second floor to the attic and maid's quarters.

> "The attic has a room with six small cots, thin mattress rolled up and pillow on it on each cot, metal nightstand beside each bed with washbasin, cup, pitcher and soap dish. There was a chamber pot under the foot of the bed. There were six hooks on the wall at the foot of the cots." - Doris Quibell

When the home received its heritage designation, one of the mentioned features was the "coat rods with numbers in the attic. These coat rods were used by First World War soldiers to hang their coats. While this feature is not designated, it is mentioned here due to its historical significance."

It's also possible this space was set up as an infirmary, and there's a rumour the space was used to house prisoners of war.

Myrtle Nasmyth McTear loved to go to the attic to see "so many treasures, so many things of my grandmothers." (Post 1980) Her grandmother was Jane Primrose Nasmyth.

Enzo Gentile used the area above the front door for prayer and had hoped to finish the space as a prayer room.

The attic was unfinished until after 1972, when Jack Gordon moved into the house. "I used to sleep up here," Jack said in a 1980 interview. He lived in the house with his sister Jean, her husband Don McInnes, and their two daughters, Lorraine and Elizabeth. After the cottage was removed from the property, any maids, domestic help, or stable hands would have lived in the unfinished attic with its open floor plan.

It seems the cots and pegs were added after the Nasmyths' time, perhaps during the Porter's time. It's rumoured that Kate Porter took in travellers.

Basement

The basement is mostly unfinished with an indoor cistern. Doris Quibell remembered the entire basement filled with medical equipment and evidence of a former kitchen in the basement.

There was a room with thick stone walls that was probably the icebox.

At the centre of basement is a room constructed of stone walls with a door and a small window. No one seems to know the purpose of the window. Could the room have had a purpose of the former doctors who resided in the house?

Along one wall is an indented space with a raised, dirt-filled bed. This is another mystery of the basement. Could this space have been used for amputations, surgeries or autopsies?

There were many deaths in the house, given the many patients that were treated by the doctors over the years. Naturally, there have been reports of ghosts and unnatural feelings.

Ghost Stories

Some have reported seeing a lady from the Victorian era wearing a red dress, but since red wasn't a colour worn during that time, Paulette wondered if perhaps the ghost was actually in white with the ruby flash glass casting a red glow. Of course, red is also the colour of blood, and one wonders if this particular ghost was an unfortunate patient of one of the doctors.

Others have reported seeing a Victorian couple wandering through the house, and this immediately brings to mind Elizabeth and William Allan as that couple, or Jane Primrose and John Nasmyth.

"I didn't like the one bedroom upstairs. I felt like I wasn't alone in the room, so if I went upstairs and the door was open, I would shut it. I guess that would keep me safe." - Doris Quibell

Christmas at the Manor

Christmas at Primrose Hill Manor included an abundance of decorated trees and garlands, and of course, house tours.

In 2023, Primrose Hill Manor was featured in the Indigo Holiday campaign. In the month of July, the house was dressed for Christmas and served as the backdrop for holiday merchandise.

The Allan family

LIVED IN THE HOUSE 1885 - 1892

Dr. William Allan was born in Fogo, Berwick, Scotland on 8 October 1858 to parents Thomas Allan and Janet Edward Bonnar. By 1861, at the age of 67, Thomas was a retired paymaster and current farmer of 912 acres, employing sixteen men and three boys. He also employed three women as house servants. The Allan family lived at Fogorig Farm, in an enormous stone house that is now a protected historic building, though severed from the farm and farm buildings.

The local church at Fogo (a word that is thought to be a portmanteau of fog and hollow), was established in the 1200 as the Priory of St. Nicholas. Among other things, St. Nicholas is the patron saint of sailors, merchants, unmarried people, students in various cities and countries around Europe, and it's easy to see these intersect with William Allan's life.

William and his younger brother Robert Thomas both lived away from home to attend school at the Wellfield House in Dunse, Berwickshire (now spelled Duns), a distance of about five miles from home. They were aged 12 and 10 respectively on the 1870 Census when they were there with other pupils. Later, they both attended medical school at the University of Edinburgh. William graduated in 1880 and Robert Thomas in 1886.

William and Robert likely decided to move to Canada because their father had already done so.

In 1834, Thomas Allan, recently retired from the Royal Navy, was granted 200 acres from the Crown over in Seymour township near Campbellford, Ontario. He bought another 900 acres and began building a village called Allandale. He constructed a steam-powered mill with an impressive 60-foot chimney since the area was without a river to power a traditional mill. He ended up naming the area Fogorig after his home village, Fogo, in Scotland, and Rig, the Scottish word for ridge. He hired 30 men to clear the forests and built a general store that also served as the first church. He planned to sell off 200-acre parcels to farmers.

While Thomas was in Canada building his empire, his wife was back home in Scotland raising William and Robert, though Thomas made frequent visits until Thomas's death in 1889 in Scotland, where he is buried.

Fogorig still stands today. On a stone plaque in the old mill's stone wall is written, "Fogorig – Built by TA- RN – Acquired A.D. 1834." Today, the old stone buildings are the site of Fogorig Brewery.

Dr. Robert Allan

Robert met Jean Letitia Esdale Shiels and married her in London, England on 23 January 1883. Her father was William Shiels, a pioneer of San Francisco, where he settled in 1850 and operated one of the first lodgings there. He went on to become owner of several properties, including a theatre, and became a millionaire. When William Shiels died in 1895, he split his wealth among his children, which meant Jean inherited about a seventh of a million, or in today's equivalency, $5,000,000.

From 1905 to 1919, Dr. Robert had a cottage at Sturgeon Point, which is a very upper-class Victorian cottage village on the north side of Sturgeon Lake. "The cottagers are divided in opinion as to the relative beauties of the two handsome boat houses erected this season by Mr. J. W. Flavelle, of Toronto, and Dr. Robt. Allan, of California. The former is of the pavilion type, and its shingled pillars, wide verandas, and rustic tint combine to produce a truly splendid effect. Dr. Allan's building is a dainty creation, the colour scheme a dark green with white trimmings, and it looks so inviting that passers-by involuntarily exclaim, "Wouldn't it be nice to live there." That's just what the Dr. intends doing, the upper flat being designed with that objective in view. He will move in shortly."

Dr. Allan and his boathouse. Photo taken by Edith Stewart after 1908.

Victorian pastimes at the cottage included boat races, regattas, and such. In October 1901, the Post reported Dr. William Allan "can handle the gun as well as most experts. As evidence of this fact, he succeeded in killing a beautiful large eagle at Sturgeon Point early on Tuesday. The bird measures over seven feet from tip to tip, and the doctor naturally feels proud of his trophy. The eagle will be mounted and will help to adorn the parlour of the doctor's fine residence."

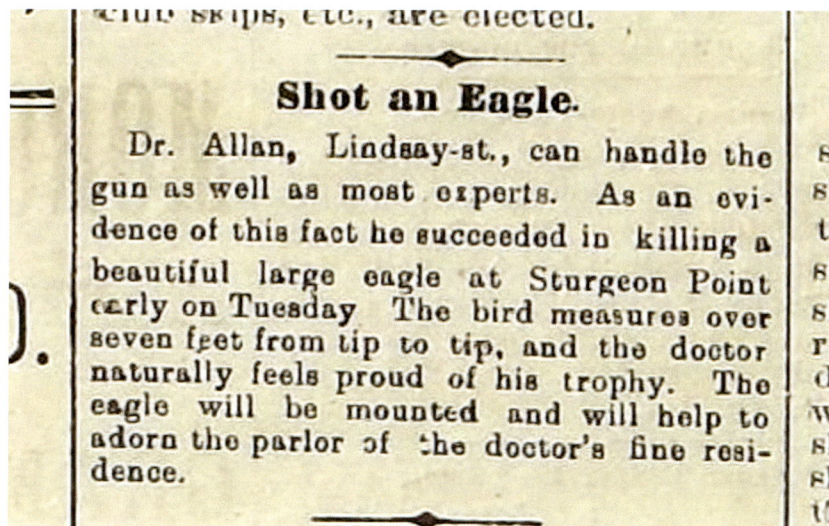

Shot an Eagle.

Dr. Allan, Lindsay-st., can handle the gun as well as most experts. As an evidence of this fact he succeeded in killing a beautiful large eagle at Sturgeon Point early on Tuesday The bird measures over seven feet from tip to tip, and the doctor naturally feels proud of his trophy. The eagle will be mounted and will help to adorn the parlor of the doctor's fine residence.

The Lindsay Post, 1901 October 11.

Robert and Jean moved to California in 1887, had four children, and lived most of their lives in Redlands, California. In 1923, Robert died in Los Angeles.

Dr. William Allan

On 12 April 1882 in Alliston, Ontario, William Allan married Elizabeth Grant Kirkland, who was born 1 March 1863 in Toronto. Although the marriage registration names John Kirkland as her father, this turns out to be incorrect. Her parents were Alexander Muir Kirkland and Matilda Fraser, and she's shown living with them on the 1871 Census as "Bessie." By 1881, her parents were living with her sister, Mary Helen Winnifred, who would go on to marry Frank Edward Joselin.

William and Elizabeth Allan moved to Janetville when they purchased the property in December 1884, one year after the birth of their first child, Moretta. Throughout 1885, Allan was building the Doctor's House, but by December, their second child was born, Mary May. Three years later, their first son arrived, Robert Thomas, and in 1899, their youngest, Charles James was born in Lindsay.

The Lindsay Post reported "Dr. Wm. Allan" built the house "at a cost of $12,000," an equivalent to $400,000 today. Construction occurred throughout 1885. In 1886, Elizabeth's parents were visiting the newly constructed house, when her father passed away. His death registration shows he died in Janetville and that Dr. William Allan was his attending physician.

Dr. Allan was coroner for the United Counties of Durham and Northumberland. After the 1890 fire destroyed the University of Toronto, Dr. William Allan of Janetville made a donation towards the rebuilding. They were clearly community-minded and generous.

In August 1892, the Belleville Intelligencer reporting on the fraud committed by Arthur O'Leary, included a side note about another financial crime committed in Lindsay– this one by Thomas B. Dean, son of County Judge William W. Dean. It seems Thomas was once the manager of the Dominion Bank in Lindsay, but was discharged from his employment "some time ago" for unknown reasons. He was "next heard of when arrested at Lockport, N.Y., on a charge of attempting to smuggle opium." While he was under arrest, his record was looked into and some interesting facts came to light, including money he borrowed and didn't pay back. And this: "A physician of Janetville, a Dr. Allen, entrusted Dean with $7000 of unregistered bonds for safe keeping. The bonds are gone, and an endeavour is now being made to recover their value from the bank."

Photo from William Allan's application for Seaman's Certificate of American Citizenship, 1922.

This article appeared in the August 5 edition of the Intelligencer, but Allan had already sold the house in July 1892 to Jane Primrose Nasmyth. The Janetville reporter for the Warder wrote, "We are going to lose our genial and respected Dr. Allan. He has sold his big house and practice to Dr. Nesmith [sic]. Ill health of Mrs. Allan being the cause of his departure from among us is deeply regretted."

In 1893 the Allan case was tried in Toronto and reported in the Canadian Post. "Dr. Allan of Janetville, and his brother, in 1888 left with Mr. T. B. Dean, a former agent of the Lindsay branch of the bank, a debenture for $7000, and Mr. Dean gave the Allans a receipt for it, the receipt being signed by Dean as agent of the bank." Bankers far and wide across Canada watched this case with interest because to them the matter seemed simple. So what was different here? Why wasn't the deposit repaid since the banks were insured for such cases of theft? In 1891 the Allans wanted their debenture and learned it had been used by Dean to secure an advance from a loan company. The bank knew nothing of the debenture being in their possession. They started an investigation. When Dr. Allan was questioned, he believed "that Dean would make good the debenture" and didn't wish "to distress him or his family." They continued to have faith in Dean, which made sense since Dean was the son of a county judge, but because of this, the judge decided Dr. Allan could no longer claim the amount of the debenture from the bank. It seems Dr. Allan had more or less admitted he knew the debenture was with Dean and therefore would be repaid by Dean– not the bank. It was a bad call on the part of the judge, freeing the bank from being responsible for their employee's actions. And since debentures are unsecured and not backed by capital, there was no way to recover the money.

JANETVILLE.

Correspondence of The Warder.

BUILDING.—Dr. Allan is about beginning operations on his new mansion. He made a bee one day last week, and 44 teams responded to the call. A large number of brick were laid on the ground but not enough to do. All could not attend, but they will when the hurry is over. We hear he is going to raise a very commodous building. We congratulate him on his enterprize.

Warder, 1885 July 31.

Dr. Allan set up his practise in Lindsay for the next few years, first at 15 E Lindsay Street South, and in 1903 at 3 and 4 E Mill Street. At both locations, the Allans were tenants. It seems likely if the stolen money had been recovered, the Allans might never have moved from Manverston Hall. Or, if they needed to relocate, they would have bought a house.

While they were in Lindsay, the Allans were socially active and continued to be community minded. In addition to William being part of the Lindsay Medical Association and the group that pushed for the construction of the Ross Memorial Hospital, in 1902 the Allans hosted the executive and members of the University of Toronto Harmonic Club when they came to perform in Lindsay as part of their Glee Club tours by invitation of the L.C.I.

Lecture Course Committee. In the letter printed in the 14 February 1902 edition of the Post, the group said they wished to "express our thanks to the committee who so kindly arranged the dance and to Dr. Allan and Mrs. Allan for their delightful hospitality."

In 1904, Dr. Allan began working aboard steamships. For his first assignment, he was appointed surgeon for the C.P.R. steamship Empress of China. The December 30 issue of the Post printed a write-up of the farewell, including a guest list that reads like a who's-who of the town's most prominent citizens:

Last Friday night the handsome dining room of the Royal held a number of Lindsays best citizens, who gathered to do honour to Dr. Wm. Allan on the eve of his departure for Vancouver, B.C., to assume his duties of surgeon on board the magnificent C.P.R. steamship Empress of China, which plies between Vancouver and the various ports of the Orient, including Tokyo and Nagasaki, Japan. Among those present were Drs. McAlpine, Gillespie, Herriman, Jeffers, White, Blanchard, Brown, Simpson, Wood, Clarke, Mayor Sootheran and, J. B. Knowlson, H. O'Leary, S.J. Bunkett, F.D. Moore, C.D. Barr, J.G. Edwards, and representatives of The Post and Watchman-Warder. Dr. McAlpine, the chairman, had at his right the guest of the evening; the vice-chair was occupied by Mayor Sootheran.

After full justice had been done the excellent bill of fare Dr. Herriman read the following address, which had been handsomely engrossed by Mr. Geo. S. Patrick, and at the proper time presented Dr. Allan with a fine Russian leather suit case of large size as a token of the esteem in which he is held by his brother medicos in town:

Sir,-- It has come to the knowledge of your conferes in Lindsay that you are about to leave this town for a more congenial field of labour. While we desire to congratulate you on your felicious change, we cannot allow you to leave us without expressing to you the esteem in which you have been held by us, not only for your gentlemanly qualities, as a man of culture, but as a skillful physician.

There is no calling or profession upon whose members larger demands are made for skill, integrity and honour than upon your own. To them are entrusted not only the comfort, health and life, but often the most sacred confidences of their client. During a very limited period of the past, science and art have made rapid strides of advancement and our profession has been no laggard. The greatest discoveries in the field of science, and the most astounding revelations of nature, have been made to contribute their rarest gems to enrich our armamentarium.

The searchlight of truth and knowledge has so altered the teachings of the past that many of our textbooks have been largely rewritten. What but recently passed as sound doctrines today are but the ghosts of our departed knowledge. Anyone in our profession, to keep abreast of the times, must be an observing and constant student. It is our very agreeable privilege to be able to say that we find you possessing all those great essentials that pre-eminently fit you for discharging the duties of your high calling.

We trust that wherever your lot may be cast you will find it pleasant to yourself and conducive to your general prosperity. We are sure you will ethically adorn your profession and merit the esteem and confidence of all with whom you may become associated.

Mr. Hugh O'Leary, on behalf of a number of citizen friends, then presented Dr. Allan with four handsome pipes in a case bearing the inscription 'Dr. Allan from Lindsay Friends, 1904.'

In his reply, Dr. Allan gave full expression to his regret at having to part from his many loyal and warm-hearted friends of Lindsay, of whose generosity and good feeling he had just received such tangible and pleasing proofs. Eloquent and witty addresses were delivered by Messrs. O'Leary, Barr, Wood, Blanchard, Sootheran, and Messrs. Needler, Knowlson, Simpson, Flavelle, Moore, Jeffers, Edwards, and others each added a few words of appreciation of Dr. Allan's good qualities and voiced their hearty regret at his pending departure.

Dr. Allan left town Saturday evening for Vancouver.

In June 1906, the Post reported that the officers and crew of the Empress of Japan honoured their surgeon, Dr. Allan with "a purse of gold" and the following remarks made by Captain Pybus:

"I have been tasked to present you with this testimonial from your shipmates on the R.M.S. Empress of Japan as an expression of the feelings of respect and affection in which you are held by all on board. I might say that these feelings are not confined alone to the European members of the ship's company, but are also shared by the Chinese crew, who are preparing a Chinese emblazoned scroll for presentation to you. Unfortunately time did not allow of its being finished before you left, but it will be forwarded in due course and will, no doubt, be a welcome addition to the similar testimonial already received by you from the Chinese passengers on our arrival in Hong Kong last voyage. In conclusion, I beg to assure you of our hearty good wishes for your future welfare."

Moretta Allan

Also in June 1906, Dr. Allan made a brief return to Lindsay for the marriage of his daughter Moretta to geologist Mowrey Bates. Bates was from New York at the time, originally from Cleveland where he was born around 1875.

The wedding took place at St. Paul's church on a Tuesday afternoon. The bride wore heavy corded silk with dainty lace trimmings. Her sister Mary May was maid of honour in green chiffon over taffeta, while the two bridesmaids, Winnifred Kirkland and Roby Hughes, daughter of Sir Sam Hughes, both wore pale pink chiffon. The groom's brother, Alex Bates, was best man, and ushers included the bride's brother, Robert Allan, Arthur Simpson (who would eventually wed Mary May Allan), F. H. Hopkins and Charles M. Squires. The bride's mother, Elizabeth Allan, wore grey lace over rose taffeta. The reception was held in the Allan house in Lindsay.

Moretta and Mowrey had one child, Francis Allan Bates, born 1909, but when Moretta died in February 1912, Francis went to live with her sister Mary May, who was single at the time. Bates went on to become an important geologist for oil companies, and none of his official biographies mention his first wife or child.

Mary May Allan

Mary May married Arthur George Simpson on 1 May 1918 in New York, though they knew each other from the days when the Allans lived in Lindsay. Simpson was a salesman born in Toronto on 10 December 1882. As an infant he briefly lived in Fenelon Falls and Bobcaygeon before his parents settled in Lindsay. He attended public school in Lindsay and then Lindsay Collegiate Institute. His father ran the Simpson Hotel at the corner of Kent and York streets, and when his father passed away, Arthur took over the business for years until he sold it and moved to Toronto. For a while he was head of a sales agency that sold motor oils, and then he became the Ontario representative for the John Gaunt Toy Co. He was into sports, and while he lived in Lindsay he was associated with the hockey club and managed the Lindsay Midgets team. Simpson was instrumental in bringing rugby to Lindsay and became manager of the team. The Post remembered Simpson as a "young man of affable disposition, happy and pleasant at all times, and had a genial handshake for all his friends and acquaintances." His death was sudden and unexpected at his home at 15 Gothic Avenue in Toronto in November 1924 at the age of 42.

Although adopted, Francis was the Simpsons' only child. They lived in Toronto until Arthur's death in 1924, after which time, Mary and Francis went to live with her brother Charles in California. Francis Allan Bates married Clara May, and they had one child, James (1944-2013). Francis died in 1951 in Contra Costa, California.

Robert Thomas Allan

Robert Thomas Allan, named for his uncle, was born at Manverston Hall on 23 February 1888. Rob attended Upper Canada College from 1905-1907. In the winter of 1903, he was in an accident that had permanent consequences. The Post reported he "was sleigh-riding in the yard when he bumped against an urn, used for flowers, and before he could get out of the way it fell on his foot, amputating one toe and injuring another one badly." The accident resulted in the partial loss of the big toe and full loss of the second toe on his right foot, as documented on the medical records in his First World War file.

He was already living in California when the First World War broke out. He completed his Canadian attestation papers in 1917 with his U.S. address and listing his father as his next of kin. Rob left his job as a broker agent mining in California to enlist with the 50th Gordons in B.C.. His brother Charles James enlisted at the same time and place. Like his brother, after basic training, Rob was assigned to the 2nd Depot Battalion B.C. Regiment of the Canadian Expeditionary Force and ranked Lance Corporal. Once in England, the brothers went to the 1st Canadian Reserve Battalion, then to the 72nd Battalion, then they were sent to France where they transferred to the 29th Canadian Infantry Battalion on 2 April 1918. Sixteen days later, the #5 Canadian Field Ambulance transported Rob to hospital for a gunshot wound to the head. Two days later, he was put back in service. On March 3, 1919, he was discharged due to demobilization.

On his return home after the war, he went back to California and applied for naturalization citizenship in 1919. A year later he married Annie Marie Monteagle in Berkeley, California on 31 July 1920, but by 1928 they were divorced. By 1930, Robert remarried, this time to Mable Francis Carr. Census data tells us he worked in sales advertising. He died in California in 1967.

Charles James Allan

Charles James lived with his mother and sister in 1911, but by 1917, he was living with his brother Robert in California. Both listed the same address on their attestation papers: 5828 Ocean View Drive in Oakland, California. Both listed their father as their next of kin with a New York address. Charles James served as a Lance Corporal for the Canadian Expeditionary Force out of Victoria, British Columbia. He signed up with the 50th Gordons and then for battle was assigned to the 2nd Depot Battalion B.C. Regiment. He served in the theatre of war in France with the 29th Canadian Infantry Battalion. When he returned in 1919, discharged due to demobilization, he returned to live in California.

In 1931, Charles was living with his sister May and her son/nephew Francis Allan Bates. On 14 August 1934, Charles James married Mary Hill Acuff from Macon, Missouri, in Tijuana, Mexico. In 1942 he was drafted into the Second World War and applied for naturalized citizenship around the same time. On 30 November 1953, Mary died. She and Charles had no children.

Dr. Allan - the later years

As for Dr. William Allan's wife Elizabeth, it's not known exactly what happened to her after the 1911 Canadian Census that shows she was living in Toronto with Mary May and Charles James. Her marital status is married, but William is not listed with them on the census. He was likely working on a ship.

In 1917, William applied for naturalization citizenship with the United States. In his application he states he is a widower and that Elizabeth is deceased. Although there are blanks to fill in for the date of Elizabeth's death, they are empty. He lists his three living children, "May" in Canada and Robert and "James" in California. Digging deeper into the military records for Robert and James shows that where the forms asked if their mother was living, they wrote 'No'. The forms were signed in July 1917, and Charles lied about his birth year. He wrote 1898 when his true birth year was 1899. It's possible he waited until after his mother's death to enlist. We do know that she was ill, as stated in the newspaper for the reason the family moved to Lindsay. We also know May did not marry her longtime sweetheart until 1918, a year after her brothers enlisted. It seems likely that May, Robert and Charles James were looking after their ill mother until 1917.

While Elizabeth's father, mother, sister and brother-in-law are all buried together at the Toronto Necropolis, the date and location of Elizabeth's death remain a mystery.

In his naturalization application, William says he arrived in the United States from Victoria, B.C. on 13 December 1907 at San Francisco aboard the vessel *Sierra*. His address at the time of the application was 136 West 79th Street in New York, an apartment building, though he likely didn't spend much time there, as for many years he served as ship's surgeon for the *Minnekahda*, a passenger ship that brought immigrants to the United States. Sometimes his address was the office of the ship company he was working for. On the attestation papers for his son, Charles James, William's address is listed as 9 Broadway, home office for the White Star Line, the company most widely known for the sinking of the *Titanic*. By 1917, when Charles James was filling out his application, White Star had been acquired by the International Mercantile Marine Company, who were using 9 Broadway as an office. William was likely working on a ship for IMM and trusting the office to contact him.

On one voyage, William met Dr. Antoinetta Benzenuti in Rome when they were waiting in a line up. He couldn't speak Italian and she knew little English, but somehow, they got along well enough that when they met up again in Hamburg, Germany, he proposed and she accepted.

> "Dr. Allan, to get married, had to produce a record of his first wife's death. That took time. He thought he had all the proofs necessary when he returned recently to Hamburg. But the American and Italian consuls declined to officiate. A German registrar tied the knot."
>
> The New York Herald, 2 March 1922

In 1924, the Post reported that Dr. Allan of New York visited Janetville. No reason for his visit is given.

Drs. William and Antoinetta eventually retired to Los Angeles, and in 1939 at a rest home, William died. He was cremated. The death notice in the Los Angeles Evening News (5 December 1939) mentions that he was a retired physician and surgeon, husband of Antoinietta Allan, and father of C. J. Allan.

Although William Allan built the grandest home in all of Janetville, it was his last permanent home. He took to the seas, and left homeownership behind for good.

Genealogy:

1. William Allan, born 8 October 1858, son of Thomas Allan and Janet Edward Bonner
Married - Elizabeth Grant Kirkland, born 1 Mar 1863 Toronto, daughter of Alexander Muir Kirkland (1827 Scotland - 31 October 1886 Janetville) and Matilda Fraser (October 1950 - 24 April 1925)
   • Mary Helen Winnifred Kirkland (1879 - 1950) married Frank Edward Joselin (May 1875 - December 1959)

1.1. Moretta Allan (1883 - 1912 Feb 18)

Married - Mowrey Bates (1875 Cleveland - 17 November 1926)

1.1.1. Francis Allan Bates (1909 - 1951)

Married - Clara May (1909 - 1971)

1.1.1.1 James Bates (1944 - 2013)

1.2. Mary May Allan (5 December 1885 Janetville - 1973)

Married - Arthur George Simpson (10 December 1882 Lindsay - 16 November 1924 Toronto) Canada)

1.2.1. Adopted 1.1.1. Francis Allan Bates (1909 - 1951) in 1912

1.3. Robert Thomas Allan (23 February 1888 Janetville - 1967 California)

Married - 31 July 1920 - Annie Marie Monteagle (1900 - 1982)

Divorced by 1928

Married by 1930 - Mable Francis Carr Fitch (1890 - 1956) - she had 2 children from previous marriage

1.4. Charles James Allan (8 December 1899 Lindsay - 6 March 1971 California)

Married - 1934 - Mary Hill Acuff (18 May 1905 Macon, MO - 30 November 1953 California)

2. Robert Thomas Allan, born 2 June 1860

Married 23 January 1883 in London, England - Jeanie Letitia Esdale Shiels (1859 California - Aug 1946 California)

2.1. William T. Lyn Allan (1884 Germany - 1946)

2.2. Esdale Allan (1886 - 1955)

Married - Edwin Shapely

2.3. Marjorie Belle Allan (1889 - 1976)

Married - James Alexander O'Connor

2.4. Ronald Shiels Allan (1897 - 1942)

The Nasmyth family

LIVED IN THE HOUSE 1892 - 1906

Jane Primrose Nasmyth

Jane Primrose Nasmyth was born on 25 February 1831 in Alloway, Scotland to parents David Morrison and Janet Wylie. David's parents were John Morrison and Janet Forrester. Janet Wylie's parents were Robert Wylie and Jean Primrose (daughter of David Primrose and Isabel Kilgowr). Robert was a ship owner.

John and Jane Primrose Nasmyth and William Wylie. Photos originally appeared in The Way We Were. William J. Edwards. Boston Mills Press. 1979.

Janet Wylie was niece to Sir James Wylie, a Baronet and physician who served as a battlefield surgeon and became known for his medical treatments for the military. He also became a court surgeon in the Russian Empire, and was knighted by Prince Regent George IV at the request of Tsar Alexander I. There's a sculpture of Sir James Wylie at the Medical and Surgical Academy in Saint Petersburg, and novelist Leo Tolstoy depicted Wylie in his door-stopper, *War and Peace*, immortalizing him with the Russian spelling of his name, Villiers.

David Morrison and Janet Wylie married 18 February 1830 in Alloa, Clackmannan, Scotland. David managed a distillery and with his wife, they had four children: Jane Primrose, John Morrison, Jessie Forrester, and David Robert. The family was living in Scotland in 1851 according to the census, but they also appear on the 1851 census in Canada. This is because the 1851 census for Canada was actually taken on 12 January 1852. The Scotland census was taken in March, so this means the Morrison family moved to Canada after March 1851 and before 12 January 1852. David had retired from the distillery. On the 1852 Census he's listed as a farmer, but by 1861 he was a "gentleman" in Montreal.

A few years after the Morrisons settled in Montreal, on 7 January 1854, Jane Primrose married John Nasmyth in Montreal, and after the wedding they moved to Mount Forest, Ontario.

John Nasmyth (I)

John Nasmyth was born on 7 April 1823 in Glasgow, Scotland to parents George Nasmyth and Margaret White. In 1931 the Nasmyths emigrated to Canada with their three children. They lived in Quebec, where they had two more children, and George worked as a farmer near Montreal and later near Danville.

When John Nasmyth was 19, he began working on the construction of the railroad for various early railway companies, beginning with the Grand Trunk East from Montreal. It appears he may have received land as part of his wages since the Crown granted him lot number 6 on the west side of Normanby Street, Mount Forest, Grey County.

In 1855, the newly married John and Jane Primrose settled in Mount Forest, where he operated a general store for nearly twenty years, while they raised their large family. He was featured in the Poetical Directory of Business published about 1863:

John Naismith, proprietor of the Glasgow House, west end of Main Street, deals in Dry Goods, Hardware, Boots, Shoes and Ready-made Clothing; pays cash for all kinds of Merchantable Produce at all hours.
Old Scotia attention and Canada bore,
You need not go naked, in rags, or forlorn,
Naismith has made-clothing to dress men complete,
Coats, pants and fine waist coats, and boots for the feet.
He is constantly selling and sending away
For all ladies' fancy in splendid array;
Dry goods are bill total body corporate in mass,
Groceries, crockery, hardware and glass;
Keep silks, and fine satins, and cambries snow white,

Prints, plaids of fast colors, both dark shade and light;
Keeps fishes and dishes, rice, coffee and teas—
Domestic and foreign each side of the seas.

One of Jane Primrose's relatives, William Wylie, a former trans-Atlantic sea captain, lived with them for a while and worked in the general store.

Naismith was also a village councillor from 1863 to 1866, and the first village reeve. He was one of many to sign the declaration that enacted the formation of a public library for Mount Forest.

Jane Primrose and John Nasmyth had eight children in Mount Forest. Unfortunately, their sons Robert and George only lived to be about ten years old.

Eldest son David remembers being 15 years old and writing his father's tenders for the railroad contracts. "It was for $500,000 of grading. How well I know it. I also wrote his tender for the road from Palmerston to Durham for $128,000." The tenders for work encompassed clearing, grading, fencing, bridging, track laying, and turn-table building. John Nasmyth was awarded many contracts in the area, including lines from Kenilworth to Mount Forest, and from Palmerston to Durham. Since this work was taking more and more of his time, in November 1870, he sold his general store in order to devote more of his time to the construction of the Toronto Grey and Bruce Railway. His contracts included the completion of the lines between Weston and Toronto, the lines between Chatham and Stoney Point, and the lines from Flesherton to Lake Simcoe.

After their youngest son James was born in August of 1874, John briefly shifted into politics. He ran in the January 1875 election, but not as a member of the Central Reform Association. He ran independently. The newspaper roasted him for this decision:

> "Mr. John Naismith, late of the village of Mount Forest, but now of the village of Weston, has just arrived in town soliciting votes as an Independent candidate aspiring to a seat for the Legislature of Ontario. Mr. Naismith has always been known in this section as a good Reformer, and it is much to be regretted that he should damage the fair reputation that he has earned by allowing himself to be made a fool in the hands of designing men. For some days back reports had been circulating throughout the riding that Mr. Naismith intended to become an Independent candidate, but Reformers generally gave no credit to such rumours. However, time has brought Mr. Naismith amongst us soliciting our suffrages, and time will also show him that he was a foolish man, but perhaps not until he has become the rejected of South Grey, for certainly Mr. Naismith's prospects of election are anything but fair."
>
> Globe 1875

Nasmyth lost the election for the Grey South riding to J.H. Hunter. The paper suggests the Nasmyths had relocated to the village of Weston, which became part of Toronto, but the 1881 Census shows John and Jane Primrose still living on their farm in Egremont township with six of their children, the family now shifting to farming while John completed railway contracts. Most of the farming was handled by eldest son, David, who remained at the farm when the rest of the family moved to Toronto in 1886.

By 1888, Jane Primrose's parents, David and Janet Morrison lived at 570 Jarvis Street in Toronto, where Janet died in 1888 and David died in 1890. When the 1891 census was taken, Jane Primrose and John Nasmyth were living in the Jarvis Street house. Then a year later, their daughter Margaret married, and Jane Primrose bought the Janetville mansion.

Jane Primrose was probably quite taken with the name Janetville, given that her mother's name was Janet, her mother-in-law was Janet, and she'd named one of her daughters Janet. She could have heard about the little village because it was making the news at the time with supporters trying to get funding for the railway to pass through the village. The incorporation had been signed in 1890, but the rail owners lacked the funds to proceed with construction. It wouldn't be until 1900 before the surveys began and a shovel would be put in the ground, several years after Jane Primrose died, but at the time the Nasmyths relocated, there was hope.

The Nasmyths moved to Janetville in 1892, and by that time most of their children had grown to adulthood, but their son, William Wylie Nasmyth, having graduated medical school in 1889 and finally completed his four years of professional study, made the move with them.

Over the next few years, Jane Primrose saw two of her children marry in Janetville, and several grandchildren born, but on 18 January 1895, she passed away. In her will, she left the house to her children, and in an interesting twist, the children sold the house to their father, John Nasmyth for $1. It's not known why she didn't leave the house to John in the first place– perhaps she expected to outlive him– nor is it known why the children sold the house back to their father. Three years later, John sold to his son Dr. William Wylie Nasmyth for $6000. His wife only paid $2000 for the house and property, so John pocketed an astounding profit for those days. John only lived for five more years. He died 21 April 1903.

David Nasmyth

Son David Morrison Nasmyth was newly widowed when he lived with his parents Jane Primrose and John in Toronto in 1891. He married Mary McKenzie in 1884, and a year later, she gave birth to their daughter Mary, only to die two weeks later. In 1892, David married Isabella McDonald, and they had four children. After the death of David's mother Jane Primrose, his father John moved in with David and Isabella at the farm near Holstein. In an article David sent to the Mount Forest newspaper, he said his father "took great pleasure in burning brush and stumps and trimming cedars on the little Saugeen creek that ran for over a mile across the farm, often taking a pocketful of wheat, and had the partridges so tame that his axe did not disturb them." After his father died in 1903, David moved his family to Alberta, where he was later joined by his brother William. David died in Alberta in 1950.

Margaret Nasmyth

The year of the move to Janetville, Jane Primrose's eldest daughter, Margaret White Nasmyth married an evangelist, William Slomans. Margaret completed her Bachelor of Arts degree at the University of Toronto. The university president described her as "the best lady scholar in Canada on the point of book-learning." She taught for a few years in Napanee and Harriston. Shortly after their marriage, Slomans arrived in New York where he was held on the ship for having admitted to committing the crime of theft when he lived in Western Canada. He was refused entry to the U.S., but held at New York until Margaret joined him, and then they moved to the Bahamas. He died in New York in 1910, while she died in the Bahamas in 1914.

Janet Wylie Nasmyth

Janet Wylie Nasmyth married Charles Ludlow Hartt in 1889 in Toronto. Charles was an accountant who ended up running his own auditing firm that employed many family members, including their children and granddaughters. John Charles Nasmyth Hartt was born in Toronto in 1890. He was a physician who served with the Canadian Air Service. In 1933 he was in Canada for training when he died in a car crash. He left a widow and a son. Charles Addison Hartt was born in 1893 in Missouri, while the family was there for a brief time. He married Edith Pugh and had one daughter. Evelyn May, who was also known as Mae E. and Mary E., married William Thorn and had three daughters, but by 1930, she was living alone with her two youngest daughters, while her oldest was living with Evelyn's parents, Janet and Charles. This change is interesting because on the 1930 Census, the daughters' names have all been changed to Hartt, and their father was not dead but remarried. Further, the census notes the oldest daughter is shown as being the "adopted daughter" of Janet and Charles. In fact, when she eventually married, she listed her mother as Evelyn and her father as Charles, cutting her biological father out completely.

John Nasmyth (II)

The third-born son of Jane Primrose, John (II), operated a store in Lotus. In her book on the history of the area, *The Rolling Hills*, Violet Carr said John owned "a tailor shop employing Fred Porter, William Bradburn and Matthew Swain as tailers." John was only in the area for a few years. On 22 May 1888, he married Elizabeth Mahood. They had two children: John (III) and Myrtle who were both born in Manvers township. Myrtle married F.W. McTear. John (II) served in the First World War as captain with the 187th Battalion of Calgary. For a number of years he operated a store in Lotus, and then went on to live in Lindsay, Montreal, and out west in Victoria and Edmonton. It appears he took up railroad contracts, like his father. He died in Quebec in 1953.

James Thomas Hutchinson Nasmyth

Jane Primrose's youngest child was James Thomas Hutchinson Nasmyth. He married Emma Armstrong in 1896 at Janetville, and moved the Ontario Gothic cottage house from the property to Lotus in 1897, though they only lived there for a couple of years. In 1900, he joined the 46th Durham Regiment, while also working as an insurance agent in Lindsay. He trained at the Stanley Barracks in Toronto, where he achieved the rank of Lieutenant two years later. In 1912, he was promoted to Captain. When the First World War broke out, he volunteered for service and was appointed Lieutenant for the 10th Battalion. He served with the Expeditionary Force in France and Flanders, at the front line, where he was promoted to Captain. During the attack on St. Julien, the heroic stand of the Canadians at the beginning of the Second Battle of Ypres, his brother Major William Wylie Nasmyth took a bullet through his lung. During the skirmish and nearly by William's side, James was killed. He was buried at Ypres, West Flanders, Belgium. Emma and James did not have children.

Dr. William Wylie Nasmyth

William Wylie Nasmyth was born in Mount Forest on 5 January 1866. He completed his physician training at Trinity Medical College in 1888, and then completed a certification in military training with the Royal School of Infantry a year later. He married Helen Carlyle Ecroyd on 27 December 1894, just two years after moving to Janetville with his parents. Helen was also born and raised in Mount Forest; they were cousins. William and Helen continued to use the name Manverston Hall, and while living here they had two children: Alfred Wylie Nasmyth was born in 1896 and Margaret Primrose Nasmyth was born 24 November 1900.

Dr. Nasmyth showed horses at the Lindsay Central fair, where he was a frequent prize winner.

The Nasmyths were known for their lawn parties at Manverston Hall. Such parties were often for the benefit of the Presbyterian church or other local cause. Activities included lawn tennis and croquet. Afternoon tea with strawberries was served along with ice cream and other refreshments. A brass band would perform for the afternoon—sometimes this was the Sylvester band from Lindsay— and more music and entertainment would follow in the evening.

Dr. Nasmyth brought the telephone to Janetville. In April and June 1897, the Watchman-Warder reported on the progress of the line that was to stretch from Janetville to Pontypool via Burton, Lotus and Ballyduff. When she toured the Janetville mansion in 1980, Myrtle McTear, niece to Dr. Naysmith, recalled there was a telephone line that connected the house to her father's store in Lotus.

William and Helen sold the house in December 1906 to Dr. John McCulloch, and in 1907, they were living in Detroit. William remained active with the military and served with distinction with the Royal Canadian Regiment during the South African war. On his return, he established his practice in Windsor, but by 1909, William was a surgeon out west in Youngstown, Alberta– but the rest of the family had yet to join him. Margaret tragically died of tonsillitis on 11 July 1909 at the Janetville house while her father was out west. Her attending physician was the new owner of the mansion, Dr. James Linton Johnston.

In Alberta, William was commanding officer of the local 89th Battalion, known as Nasmyth's Nonpareils, a unit that was much loved by Albertans. When the First World War broke out in 1914, William gave up his medical practice and was given command of a battalion that became known as the "Fighting Tenth." When William went overseas with his battalion, Helen went with him to England where she aided the war effort.

In 1915, while William was fighting at the front lines of Belgium, he was shot through the lungs and at his side was his brother James, killed in action. The Lindsay Post reported, "the wounded major refused to allow himself to be carried from the field until his men had all been cared for." William miraculously survived and was sent home.

He did not give up. He was given the task of recruiting for the 89th Battalion, and by April 1916, he once again headed back to war– this time with his son Alfred, a new recruit. The battalion was sent off with cheers from the crowd of thousands at the depot platform. The Lacombe Guardian reported, "They were a likely-looking lot, these young Alberta volunteers. The military training they had undergone, the route marches they had performed, the physical drill that had been their daily morning task for weeks, had borne its effect, and Nysmyth's Nonpareils looked as fine a type of fighting soldier as any part of the British Empire could produce."

On arrival, the troops were split up and used as reinforcements. William, now a Lt-Col., was assigned to the Canadian Army Medical Corps.

Alfred, only 20 years old, spent six more months training before he was transferred to 9th Battalion with the Royal Flying Corps, as a Flying Officer Observer at the rank of Lieutenant. He was assigned to the Alberta

Regiment Depot in May of 1917 and then sent to France in October, at the height of the Battle of Passchendaele. On October 6 Alfred arrived for duty in France. On October 12, Alfred was sent out as part of 66 Squadron in an offensive attack to provide support for the ground troops against the advancing Germans. It was a day of heavy rain, and in the end, heavy losses. Three of the squadron's planes were shot down: 2Lt Martin Newcomb, 2Lt Robert William Brownlee, and Alfred.

Four days later Alfred was reported as "missing" in his record. Nearly a month went by, then, German forces dropped a message across the Allied lines saying Newcomb and Matthewson survived their crashes, but were now held prisoner, and Alfred was dead. The Battle of Passchendaele ended when the area was captured by the Canadian Corps in November 1917, just a few weeks after Alfred was shot down.

Nearly a year later, a note was added to Alfred's record stating that he was now "presumed dead." Germans reportedly buried him in Lauwe German Military Cemetery in Belgium, plot 5, row c, grave 9. In 1922, a further note was added to his record: "Now for official purposes. Killed in action 12/10/17." (After the Second World War, the bodies at Lauwe were moved to Menen, Belgium, where 48,000 German soldiers were buried from the First World War.)

After the war, William returned to Alberta to live with Helen, and by 1925, they were living in Sylvan Lake, where he carried on his practice and a drug store. Helen died in 1928, and in 1941, William followed her. He received full military honours at his funeral. The casket was carried on a gun carriage that was drawn by a Jeep. There was a firing party and a trumpeter who played the Last Post and the Rouse.

When asked to contribute some encouraging words for the book, *On Active Service: a book of golden thoughts* (1918), William submitted this poem by Tennyson:

> *Ye, but all good things await*
> *Him who cares not to be great,*
> *But as he serves or serves the state,*
> *Not once or twice in our rough Island story,*
> *The path of duty was the way to glory.*

Genealogy:

George Nasmyth and Margaret White:

1.0.. George Nasmyth (1797 Lesmahagow, Scotland - 1867)
    Married Margaret White (1791 Bathgate, Scotland - 1871)
    1.1 Margaret

Married John Greenshields
1.2 John
Married Jane Primrose Morrison
See below.
1.3 Agnes
Married in 1871 to William Gruer
1.3.1 Maggie
1.4 George
Married Caroline
1.4.1 Jane P
1.4.2 George
1.4.3 Margaret
1.5 Mary
Married Dr. Alfred Erspert Eckroyd
1.5.1 William N.
1.5.2 Helen Carlyle
1.5.3. Mary
1.5.4. Henrietta

John Nasmyth and Jane Primrose Morrison

1. Jane Primrose Morrison, (25 Feb 1831 Alloway, Scotland - 18 January 1895 Janetville), parents David and Janet Morrison

Married 7 January 1854 - John Nasmyth (1823 - July 1903), parents George Naismith (1797-1867) and Margaret White (1791-1871)

    1.1. Robert Nasmyth (1857 - 10 June 1867)

    1.2. David Morrison Nasmyth (1860 April - 1950)

    Married 25 June 1884 - Mary McKenzie (1862 - 1885)

    1.2.1. Mary McKenzie (1885 - 1966)

    Married - Isabella McDonald (1857 - 1938)

    1.2.2. John Darby (1893 - 1968)

    1.2.3. Phoebe (1895 - 1903)

    1.2.4. Peter David (1897 - 1991)

    1.2.5. Joseph James (1900 - 1954)

    1.3. Margaret (Maggie) White Nasmyth (1862 - 1914 Bahamas)

    Married 1892 - William Slomans (1862 - 1910)

    1.4. John Nasmyth (1864 Mount Forest - 1 November 1952 Hemmingford, QC)

    Married 22 May 1888 - Elizabeth Mahood (1863 - 1951)

    1.4.1. John (1889 Manvers - 1936)

    1.4.2. Myrtle (1892 Manvers - 1983 Lindsay)

    1.5. William Wylie Nasmyth (1866 - 1941)

    Married 27 December 1894 - Helen Carlyle Ecroyd (1867 - 1928 Red Deer)

    1.5.1. Alfred Wylie Nasmyth (1896 - 1917)

    1.5.2. Margaret "Marjorie" Primrose Nasmyth (1900 November 24 - 1909 July 11 Janetville)

1.6. George Nasmyth (1868 - 1873 January 27)

1.7. Janet Wylie Nasmyth (1870 - 1954)

Married Charles Ludlow Hartt of St. Louis, moved to East Liverpool, Ohio.

1.7.1 John Charles Nasmyth Hartt (1890 Toronto - 1933 Canada, car accident, buried in Ohio) served with Canadian Air Service

Married Irene/Grace

1.7.1.1. Richard Hartt

1.7.2 Charles Addison Hartt (1893 May 10 Missouri - 21 November 1892 Ohio)

Married 28 June 1925 West Virginia - Edith Anita Pugh

1.7.2.1. Barbara Hartt

1.7.3 Evelyn May (also Mae E, Mary E.)

Married William Thorne, then divorced.

1.7.3.1. Shirley May (adopted by Janet and Charles Hartt)

1.7.3.2. Marjorie J.

1.7.3.3. Muriel Janette

1.8. James Thomas Hutchinson Nasmyth (23 August 1873 - 1915 killed in action buried at Ypres, West Flanders, Belgium)

Married 20 October 1896 at Janetville - Emma Amelia Armstrong (16 January 1872 Janetville - 30 December 1953 Lindsay), daughter of Christopher and Jeannie Armstrong. No children.

The McCulloch family

LIVED IN THE HOUSE 1906 - 190

Dr. John McCulloch graduated Queen's Medical College in 1901 and already had a practise in Lindsay when he purchased the Doctor's House in Janetville and relocated there in December 1906. This was an unpopular move, as for every week of 1907 and right up until the end of May 1908, an ad ran in the Lindsay Post telling readers he'd moved to Janetville, but at the urging of his patients, he would make the trip to Lindsay one day a week.

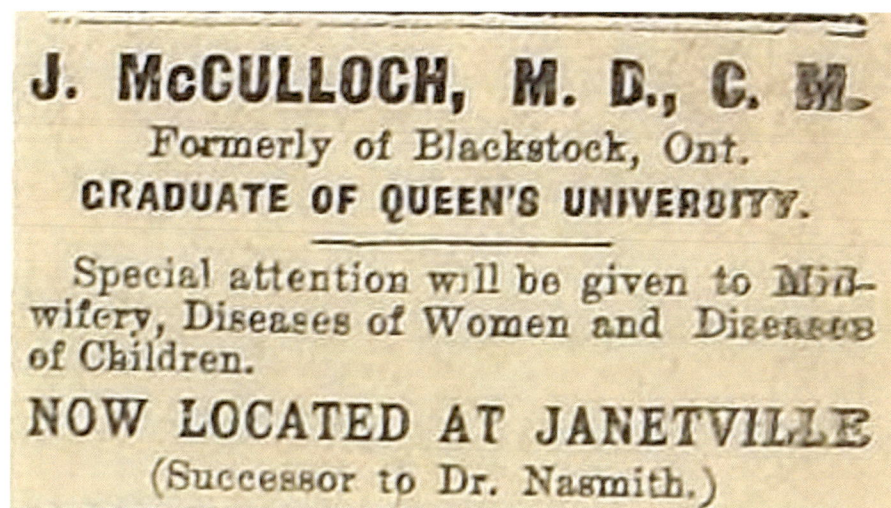

J. McCULLOCH, M. D., C. M.
Formerly of Blackstock, Ont.
GRADUATE OF QUEEN'S UNIVERSITY.

Special attention will be given to Mid-wifery, Diseases of Women and Diseases of Children.

NOW LOCATED AT JANETVILLE
(Successor to Dr. Nasmith.)

The weekly commute clearly became too much, and business was better in Lindsay, for in June 1908, McCulloch returned to Lindsay to live in the house on Cambridge Street, formerly occupied by Dr. Herriman. A few years later, Dr. McCulloch set up his practice in an office on William Street North, across from the Post, and moved his residence to a house on Sussex Street North.

John McCulloch was born in Darlington township on 19 March 1872 to parents George McCulloch and Ellen/Eleanor Smith. After graduating medical school, he married Sara Jane McFadyen on 15 October 1902, daughter of Neil McFadyen, born in Sunderland. They had two children: Neil John George McCulloch, born 10 June 1904 in Lindsay, who became an insurance agent in Lindsay, and Hugh Locklin McCulloch, born 1908 at the Janetville house, who became a banker in California.

John's mother, Eleanor McCulloch, remarried to Robert McLaughlin in 1901, the same year McLaughlin incorporated his McLaughlin Carriage Company. His son, Colonel R.S. "Sam" McLaughlin, who started the McLaughlin Motor Car Company that became General Motors of Canada, became Dr. McCulloch's step-brother.

Dr. McCulloch's duties as a physician brought him adjacent to many tragedies, including bearing witness to the hanging sentence for Frederick McGaughey, the young man who murdered Beatrice Fee in 1924. For his crime, McGaughey was hanged in the centre courtyard at the Lindsay jail. Witnesses of the event included Sheriff Vrooman, Governor Stone, Turnkey Grozelle, Rev. F. H. McIntosh, Dr. White, Jail Surgeon, Dr. McCulloch and the representatives of the local press. It was the last hanging to occur at the Lindsay jail. McCulloch was likely a good choice for the job given his experience in the military.

On May 1, 1916, Dr. McCulloch enlisted with the 109th Battalion in Lindsay, and entered the First World War at age 44, leaving behind his wife and sons aged 12 and 8. He was transferred to the Canadian Army Medical Corps, and after a few months in the training camp, he was sent to the No. 7 Queen's University General Hospital in Étaples, France. In March 1917, he had a case of bronchitis so bad he was put on a three-week medical leave. By April 1, he was sent back to his unit– just in time to receive wounded from the Battle of Vimy Ridge.

Étaples was a major transit camp on the coast of France that at any one time sheltered 100,000 people for training or for medical services in one of the 22 hospitals. It was also the site of a mysterious respiratory illness through the years 1915 - 1916. In 2000, Steve Connor published an article in *The Independent*, stating, "John Oxford, Professor of virology at St. Bartholomew's and the Royal London School of Medicine, and his colleagues believe the Étaples camp became the birthplace of an influenza strain two years before it spread across the world with devastating effects." This means Dr. McCulloch might not have solely suffered from bronchitis, but likely had contracted what was known as the Spanish flu. Over the next few years, he was sent on multiple sick leaves to recover, but it seems he would take the disease to his grave.

On 4 October 1926, Dr. McCulloch returned to Lindsay from a trip to western Canada, after taking ill. He was reported as resting comfortably at his home at 228 Kent Street West, but two days later he died. Cause of death was officially reported as coronary thrombosis and chronic Bright's disease, but the military also officially recognized his cause of death as related to his service in the First World War. Dr. McCulloch's death made front page news, and he was given full military honours with a parade to his burial at Riverside Cemetery.

Genealogy:

1. John McCulloch (19 March 1872 Darlington twp - 6 October 1926 Lindsay), parents George McCulloch and Ellen Smith
Married 15 October 1902 - Sara Jane McFadyen (b. Sunderland - d. 8 September 1945 Lindsay), father Neil McFadyen
    1.1. Neil John George McCulloch (10 June 1904 - ?)
    1.2. Hugh Locklin McCulloch (1908 Janetville - 29 October 1973 Lindsay)

The Johnston family

Dr. James Linton Johnston bought the Janetville mansion in 1908. He was a bachelor when he bought the house, as noted on the title register, but on December 30 of that year, he married Kate Sara McLeod, a girl from his home county in eastern Ontario.

Born and raised in Fournier, Ontario, Dr. Johnston arrived in this world on 13 July 1862 to Alexander Johnston and Martha Linton. After completing his early education, he taught at local public schools for a while before pursuing higher education to become a physician. First, he graduated from medical school at McGill University in 1901, and then in May 1902, he successfully passed his exams at the Royal College of Physicians and Surgeons, of Edinburgh and Glasgow. When he returned to Canada, he spent two months in Manitoba during the summer of 1902, before studying for his Ontario licence. He passed his exams in January 1903, returned to his hometown, and set up a busy practice for the next five years.

On June 6, 1908, Dr. Johnston bought the Janetville mansion from Dr. McCullough for the princely sum of $4000. How he came to know about the house is a mystery. Perhaps Dr. McCulloch was advertising the place to alumni of medical schools. In any case, Dr. Johnston made the decision to leave his beloved hometown.

A large farewell party was held at the home of his brother Louden on Monday July 13, 1908. Sixty guests attended with musical entertainment provided by the Ladies Aid group. The event culminated in a presentation to Dr. Johnston and the following speech was made (and reprinted in the Alexandria News):

Dear Friend and Physician,

It is with the greatest regret and heart-felt sorrow that we learn of your prospective departure from our little town. While residing among us for over five years, going in and out of our homes, you have gained the undivided respect of everyone both as a man and as a physician. We have relied upon your medical skill when we were sick and we were always sure of the best attention and sympathy conscientiously given, and when sorrow visited our homes your words of sympathy and consolation made the sorrow lighter. You have always manifested an earnest devotion to duty and a hearty interest in the welfare of the community. Being in touch with us thus intimately, your absence will be more intensely felt than if our co-mingling were only in a casual manner, and while we regret parting with you the pang is softened by the knowledge that such a friendship existed. Even in your busy life your faithful and regular attendance to the church services on Sabbath has been an example to us. On behalf of the community it is our desire to express our most hearty good wishes for your continued welfare and we sincerely hope that in your new field of work you will have every happiness and success, and that kind friends will always surround your path. We commend you to God, whom we know you delight to serve and we hope that if we never meet here again, we will meet you beyond the River, where good-bye is never said and where partings are unknown.

Dr. Johnston replied with a few well-chosen words, stating that "wherever he would live in the future he did not expect to have as many kind friends as he had in Fournier." Six months after his arrival, Dr. Johnston shipped five barrels of apples "from his own orchard" to his friends in Fournier.

Dr. Johnston, of Janetville, who formerly practised here, shipped five barrels of a fine variety of apples to a number of his friends here. They were grown in his own orchard.

The News, Alexandria, ON. 1909 January 1.

As a doctor, Johnston was well loved and highly respected. He was described as having a "straight forward, honest and honourable character." He inspired confidence in his patients and "his cheerful, self-contained manner was ever a tower of strength in itself." (Alexandria News, Dec 1911)

When Dr. William Wylie Nasmyth's daughter Margaret tragically died of tonsillitis on 11 July 1909 at the Janetville house, her father was out west. She'd likely been staying with friends in Janetville intending to join her parents when she became ill. Her attending physician was Dr. Johnston, meaning Margaret likely died in the Doctor's House– the same house where she was born.

Dr. Johnston and Kate only had one child. Martha Linton Johnston, born 19 January 1910 at the Janetville house with Dr. Collison attending.

In December of the following year, Dr. Johnston suddenly became ill. He was admitted to the Ross Memorial Hospital in Lindsay, but was quickly moved to the Toronto General Hospital, where he died from a brain tumour on 20 December 1911. He was buried at the family plot in the Franklin Corners (now the Riceville United Cemetery in Prescott.) His brother held a gathering at his home in Fournier. The funeral took place on December 23 at the Methodist Church in Fournier with hundreds of his friends in attendance "to pay their last tribute of respect to the memory of the deceased" (Alexandria News, Dec 1911.) He was a much loved member of every community where he spent any time.

After Dr. Johnston's death, Kate and Martha remained in the house. Kate was active with the local Janetville Women's Institute and held meetings in her home. After the First World War, she sold the house to the Porters in December 1918. Kate and Martha spent some time living with Kate's niece, Bessie McMillan Stevenson and family in Manitoba, before moving to Los Angeles, California, where Martha attended school and later married Paul Theordore Stirn. They had one child.

Martha Linton Johnston/Johnstone.
Photo from her application for U.S. cit-
izenship, 1935.

Both Kate and Martha applied for naturalized citizenship. Their applications state that they arrived in the U.S. in 1921. Both applications show that they opted to add a letter 'E' to their last name after they moved to the U.S., though no reason is given for this change.

Kate lived until 1964 and was buried at the Forest Lawn Cemetery in Glendale, California, using the last name "Johnstone"; she did not remarry.

Genealogy:
1. James Linton Johnston (13 July 1862 - 20 December 1911 Toronto), parents Donald McLeod and Mary McMillian. He had 3 sisters and 5 brothers.
    Married 30 December 1908 - Kate Sara McLeod (27 February 1877 Laggan, ON - 30 August 1964 Los Angeles)

1.1. Martha Linton Johnston (19 January 1910 Janetville - 12 March 1990 California)
    Married Paul Theodore Stirn (1907 - 1986)
    1 child.

The Porter family

LIVED IN THE HOUSE 1918 - 1962

John Porter, born in 1829 in Cavan, was one of Manvers township's early settlers, one who cleared the wilderness from the land that he farmed for the rest of his life. For over 60 years he was married to Ann Morton, born 1832 in Cavan. They had ten children, four sons and six daughters. Their son, John James Porter, married Kate Fisher on 3 January 1899.

Catherine "Kate" Fisher was born on 9 July 1877 in Ops township, youngest of 12 children, to parents Donald Fisher and Mary Ann Margaret Reeds.

For years, John and Kate lived near Janetville on a 200-acre farm fronting the 14th line of Manvers where they worked until they retired to the Janetville mansion in December 1918.

After John passed away in 1941, Kate continued to live in the mansion until November 1962. Her nephew Stanley Fisher needed a place to live and she needed a handyman, so he lived with her. During this time, she continued to be active in the community and became affectionately known as "Aunt" Kate or Janetville's "Grand Old Lady." She was often described as kind and with a strong love of life and people. "Her sincerity and wisdom, honesty and keen sense of humour won her the admiration and respect of large numbers who were privileged to have made her acquaintance. Those who had partaken of the splendid hospitality of her home, where the welcome mat was always at the door, will never forget the pleasing experience." (Post 1964)

Doris Quibell, granddaughter of the Porters, who owned the Janetville mansion from 1918 to 1962, remembered a particular book in the library. She said this book was given to the families who lost a member to the Titanic. Unfortunately, she didn't know who the book belonged to, or if her family was related to a victim of the Titanic. She said, "Nobody talked about that book." She was perhaps referring to the book that was published following the inquest, but it was also available to the public, so it's possible an avid reader may have purchased a copy.

Genealogy:

Porter:

1. John Porter (1829 Cavan - 1916 May 5 Manvers)
   Married Ann Morton (1832 - 1918 June 6 Manvers)
   1.1. Susannah Jane Porter (1857 - ? before 1916?)
   1.2. Albert Porter (1859 July 29 - 1939 May 3 Janetville)
   Married Letitia McGill
   1.3. John James Porter (1861 -)
   1.4. Charlotte Porter (1863 - 1953 April 13 Lindsay)
   Married Thomas Deyell
   1.5. Sarah Porter (1863* - 1942 July 7 Janetville)
   *Note: death certificate documents birth date as 1886 October 23, but earlier census documents stated 1863)
   Married: William Charles Armstrong
   1.6. Elizabeth Porter (1865 - 1963 April 8 Lindsay)
   Married: William Davidson
   1.7. Martha Porter (1867 - 1950 November 15 Lindsay)
   Married: Joseph Hickson
   1.8. William Henry Porter (1872 April 18 - 1951 November 3 Ops)
   Married: Margaret Kerr
   1.9. Edith Porter (1878 August 4 - 1953 January 26 Lindsay)
   Married: Thomas Wilbert Irvine
   1.10. Wellington Porter (1879 - 1961 January 11)

Fisher:

1. Donald Daniel Fisher (1828 Scotland - 1920 April 11) parents: Duncan Fisher and Margaret McArthur
   Married: Mary Anne Margaret Reeds (? - 1912 August 24)
   1.1. Margaret Fisher (1852 - 1952 August 12)
   1.2. Mary Fisher (1854 - 1924 Fenelon Falls)
   Married: William Golden (1856 - 1954 December 5)
   1.2.1. John
   1.2.2. Minnie
   1.2.3. William
   1.2.4. Margaret
   1.3. Martha Fisher (1856 - 1929 September 9 Fenelon Falls)
   Married: William Davis (1857 December - 1925 December 31)
   1.3.1. Dan
   1.3.2. Margaret
   1.3.3. Mary Anne Ethel
   1.4. Annie Fisher (1858 July 19 - 1922 November 12 Valentia)

Married: William J. Brown (1852 - 1927 November 8)
1.4.1. Austin
1.4.2. Florence
1.4.3. John
1.4.4. Eva
1.5. Duncan Fisher (1860 - 1931)
Married: Mary Spence (1860 - 1935 June)
1.5.1 Ruby
1.5.2. Wilfred
1.5.3. Marie Grace
1.6. Jessie (Jeanette) Fisher (1862 - 1922 August 24)
Married: Alexander Wilson (1854 January 25 - 1928 July 28)
1.6.1. Lewis
1.6.2. Mary
1.6.3. Thomas
1.6.4. Margaret
1.6.5. Katherine
1.6.6. Bertha
1.6.7. Archie
1.7. Donald Fisher (1865 March 28 - 1932 May 1)
Married: Jane McGill (1878 January 2 - 1941 March 6)
1.7.1. Aldah
1.7.2. Archie
1.7.3. Arvice
1.7.4. Angus
1.7.5. Anne
1.8. Thomas Fisher (1867 - 1942 February 12)
Married: Margaret E. Wilson (1870 - 1935)
1.8.1. Donald
1.8.2. Thomas
1.8.3. Catherine
1.8.4. John
1.8.5. Bruce
1.9. Peter Fisher (1869 - 1942 March 27)
Married: Elizabeth Shackleton (1883 October 21 - 1950 March 27)
1.9.1. Thomas Melville
1.9.2. Mary
1.9.3. Edna
1.9.4. Mervin
1.10. Richard Fisher (1872 May - 1934 December 9)
Married: Florence Isabelle McGill (1881 - 1953 April 10)
1.10.1. Willard
1.11. Joseph Fisher (1875 March 10 - 1932 January 5)
Married: Lavina McGill (1885 March 23 - 1975 July 17)
1.11.1. Olive

1.12. Catherine Fisher (1877 July 9 - 1964 May 23)
Married: John James Porter (1861 January 3 - 1941 April 18)
1.12.1. Elsie

The Davis family

LIVED IN THE HOUSE 1962 - 1966

Bill Davis was an employee at General Motors in Oshawa when he bought the Janetville mansion in November 1962. He lived in the house with his parents, Carl and Ada, and his sister Shirley. At the time, his father operated a garage and service station in Westhill, a village of Scarborough. Bill told the Post, "I bought this house because both my parents and myself love the stateliness of old architecture. I intend to restore it back to its former beauty and have made a considerable start."

In the summer of 1963, the Davis family hosted a car tour that began in Windsor and proceeded to Montreal with a coffee-break stop-over at the Janetville mansion. The group of participants were members of various car clubs, including antique and vintage model clubs. Bill participated in the tour, driving his 1924 Rolls Royce.

The interest in cars ran strongly through the Davis family. Bill contributed two cars to the Oshawa antique car museum: a 1919 Gray Dort and a 1924 Rolls Royce limousine. His uncle, Lloyd John Davis designed a car.

The love of cars stemmed from Bill's grandfather, John Howard Davis, son of Robert Davis, an important pioneer ship-builder in Kingston.

Photo of Bill Davis and the mansion originally appeared in the Lindsay Post, 1963 January 9

A History of Shipbuilding and Automobile Design

Pioneer ship-builder, Robert Davis, was born near Utica, New York, around 1848. As a child, he and his brother John Davis learned the shoe-making trade. When the family moved to Wolfe Island, Robert entered the carpentry trade. He was awarded the contract to build the township hall, the Anglican church parsonage, and other buildings around the village. In 1854, Robert partnered with Zediac Wright and the two set up a shingle mill. The lumber business was booming and four years later, the pair built a steam mill. When the American Civil War ended, the demand for lumber waned, so the partners sold the business and Robert started a shipyard. Over the next several years, Robert, his wife Fannie Tipson and their young family moved to Clayton, N.Y. for six years, where Robert operated a sash and door factory while building ships on the side. Then they moved to Westport, where the growing Davis business would have connection with the Rideau Lakes. Passenger steamers were built and the business grew to become the Rideau Lakes' Navigation Company. The family returned to Wolfe Island, Robert built more buildings and ships there.

In 1880, Robert, his family and businesses moved to Kingston. They constructed a floating drydock that they operated for five years before selling it. They built a new drydock that Robert operated until three years before he died at age 88 in 1928. Robert married his second wife, Barbara Cramand, on 20 November 1878. With his first wife, Fannie, Robert had 10 children.

William Davis (far left) and Carl Davis (far right). Photo originally appeared in the Lindsay Post, 1963 July 24.

The Davis Dry Dock

Robert's shipyard business, the Davis Dry Dock Company, started life in 1867 with the completed dry dock in use by 1889. The dock is 61 metres long, 14 metres wide, and 4.3 metres deep with a timber bottom, concrete sill and sheet steel sides. It's essentially a method of moving ships out of the water for repairs or for loading freshly constructed ships into the water. The Davis family built many ships, some of them quite luxurious.

R. Davis and Sons built the steam yacht *Titanis* for Samuel Daniels of Ottawa in 1891.

Matthew Davis refitted the *Rideau King* and built the *Rideau Queen* in 1900-1901. The *Rideau Queen* was 111 feet long with staterooms for sleeping for 75 passengers. The staterooms were furnished with spring beds, snowy linens, bright carpets, marble wash-basins with running water and an early form of air-conditioning with cool air supplied from below via three-inch pipes. The ship also sported a lavish saloon with plush furniture and carpets. The highlight of the ship was the dining room, a marvel of beauty and elegance, finished in highly polished red oak, the furniture was oak, and the room's finishing touches in linen, silver and shining glassware. Every piece of glass and silver bore the name 'Rideau Queen.' The ship was built for the Rideau Lakes Navigation Company and Captain Noonan, and spent many years riding the Rideau Lakes, but as travel by automobile became more common and the ships were at the whims and mercy of the weather, steam ship travel declined. In 1915, the *Rideau Queen* was put to rest forever when water levels became too low.

The Davis Dry Dock Company also built ships and lifeboats that were used to aid the effort of the First World War.

John Howard Davis built and delivered steam launches, but he also became interested in building automobiles. Methods of transportation had started to shift from ships and on to passenger trains and automobiles. In 1924, John built a touring vehicle that was similar to the Locomobile. The sedan was assembled after hours and behind closed doors at the shipyard. It had a Red Seal Continental engine, spoked wheels from Benjamin Wheel Company, axles and springs from Gananoque Spring and Axle Col, Timken rear assembly, on a frame constructed by the Davis Dry Dock Co. It cost between $2000-$3000 to build. When it was nearly finished, it caught fire and was heavily damaged. During the summer of 1923, John's son Lloyd rebuilt the car and finished it in natural polished aluminium. He constructed it as a roadster called the 'Fleetwood-Knight'. It had a six-cylinder sleeve-valve 80 hp engine, a Stromberg carburetor, three-speed transmission, Eaton axles, and five-spoke steel artillery-type wheels with balloon tires on 20" rims.

The Fleetwood-Knight. Photo found on Wayback Machine.

Lloyd drove the 'Fleetwood-Knight' to work when he "joined General Motors as Assistant Chassis Engineer in 1927 in Oshawa. The Chief Engineer at that time spent a great deal of time going over the [Fleetwood-Knight] along with many others in the organization. The Engineer in charge of the Cadillac Division christened it "H.M.S. FURIOUS."" (www.reginaantiqueauto.ca)

Even after Lloyd sold the roadster, it was driven for many more years and over 400,000 miles until it was lost in quick-sand when it went off the road in the 1960s.

It's been speculated that the investment into the car-build put the shipyard's profits in decline, resulting in John Howard Davis leaving the family business, but there were other problems, such as the waning demand for ships and luxury yachts like the *Rideau Queen*, given the rise in popularity of automobiles and car tour vacations.

In 1928, the Davis Dry Dock Company was sold to S. Anglin and Co, ending the Davis era at this site, though the dry dock continued to be used and still exists today. Recently, there's some interest in having the site designated as historically significant.

Manita

In 1900, Bobcaygeon's Mossom M. Boyd commissioned his final steamboat, and instead of choosing a company from one of the usual shipyards in the Kawartha Lakes area (Port Perry, Port Hoover, Lindsay or Bobcaygeon), he went with the Davis Dry Dock Company in Kingston. He sent his specifications and the vessel was constructed and delivered.

The Manita at Fenelon Falls.

The *Manita* made many regular trips between Coboconk and Lindsay or between Lindsay and Bobcaygeon without issue. Then early in the morning on June 15, 1906 while docked in Bobcaygeon, fire was discovered that destroyed the decks, cabins aft of the pilot house, lifeboat, life preservers, funnel, boiler fixings, valves and gauges. The hull was intact. The vessel was restored and less than a month later, resumed its regular voyages. The *Manita* sailed its final voyage under Boyd's ownership on September 20, 1906 before it was sold and used in the Stony and Rice Lake area for the Trent Valley Navigation Company.

Phoebe

One of the most famous ships built by the Davis family company was the steam launch named *Phoebe*. She was built for John Brashear, a lens crafter and telescope builder, who was far more well-known in Pittsburgh for his work at the Allegheny Observatory. He summered in Canada around 1895 with his wife, Phoebe, because they'd been going through a rough time and friends recommended they vacation in Muskoka.

The Brashears enjoyed their time and returned year after year to a rental cottage before buying an island on Lake Muskoka in 1898. They named the island Urania. In 1901 they bought a steam launch built by the Davis Dry Dock Company and ran the boat on many trips before it was damaged by fire. Brashear's friend Andrew Carnegie presented him with a new steam launch built by the Davis family company, and John named the boat after his wife, Phoebe. The boat was much loved over the next several years until Phoebe died in 1910. Heartbroken, Brashear lost interest in boating. Then, in 1913, the boat was destroyed by fire.

During their years in Muskoka, John and Phoebe made many friends. When they heard about the steam launch's demise, they raised a pile of money and bought John a new boat and boathouse. *Phoebe II* was built by the Davis family in 1914. Matthew Davis was the chief builder.

She was 48-feet long and "equipped with a Davis-built wood-fired water-tube boiler and a 65-horsepower Davis two-cylinder steam engine... She had fine bow lines and what was called a 'canoe stern.' The enclosed forward cabin/pilot house had curved windows; the centre-section's boiler room had roll-up side curtains; the enclosed aft-cabin had washing facilities on the port side; generous fore- and aft-decks allowed passengers plenty of room outside the cabins. Mahogany panelling in both cabins reflected the taste of an age of elegance. Nickel-plated deck fittings gave a pleasing effect and a touch of elegance." (Enright 2007)

When he was 73 years of age, Brashear retired from his work and spent more time in Muskoka. The gift of his friends was cherished, and Brashear resumed boating. After Brashear died in 1920, the *Phoebe II* moved through a series of owners until 1979 when members of Kingston's Frontenac Society of Model Engineers mobilized to purchase and repatriate the steam launch. She was declared a "National Treasure" under the Cultural Properties and Heritage Act of Canada.

In the 1990s, the *Phoebe II* underwent restoration, a six-year project led by Henk Wevers, a retired Queen's University mechanical engineering professor. In 2003, a ceremony was held at the Pump House Steam Museum to mark the end of the project. Today, she is an artifact of the City of Kingston.

John Howard Davis

One of Robert's sons was John Howard Davis, born in 1872 in New York. John operated the Davis Dry Dock Company from 1923 to 1927.

John married Jennie Shanessy and they had five children: Ruth, Lloyd, Robert, Dr. Colmer, and Carl. John passed away in March 1937 just three months after the marriage of his youngest son, Carl.

Lloyd John Davis

Lloyd fell in love with cars in 1906 when he was five years old and went for a ride in a Stevens-Duryea. Lloyd explained, "Having been sufficiently fortunate to be born into a family of Boat Builders and Designers which included the manufacture of steam boilers, steam engines, gasoline engines and all types of boats, there isn't any surprise to me that I had the desire to manufacture a masterpiece to run on four wheels." (www.reginaantiqueauto.ca)

By the time he was 12, Lloyd was driving automobiles around the shipyard, and within two years, he began driving on the roads. At sixteen, he was offered a job as a driver for a wealthy family, and he spent his summer behind the wheel of a 1915 Cadillac.

A year later, Lloyd was asked to design a heavy duty truck to carry loads for the shipyard. The vehicle was completed a year later. In 1923, he began to design the Fleetwood-Knight.

Lloyd married Jessie Annette Hutton, and they had one child, Barbara. During the Second World War, Lloyd joined the Aircraft Controller's Department. He was part of the Anson Program up to the Anson Mark Five, then he was with the Mosquito Program with DeHavilland Aircraft until the end of the war. He went on to form his own general contracting business, mostly constructing industrial buildings with the exception of a few high-end custom homes. He also worked for the Toronto International Airport.

Carl Vaughn Davis

Carl, born 30 September 1912, was raised in Kingston. In January 1937, he married Ada J. Armstrong in Kingston. They had two children: William Carl Irvine and Shirley. For several years, the family lived in the Pickering area where Carl operated a garage and service station in Westhill.

The family lived in the Janetville mansion from 1962 to 1966. At the time of Carl's death in 1976, Shirley was living in Locust Hill and Bill was in Selkirk, Manitoba. The family moved to Abbotsford, B.C., where Ada passed away at age 67.

Genealogy:

1. Robert Davis born 25 October 1834 at Rome, NY to parents Mathias/Matthew Davis (1799 Wales - 1857 Mar 8 Wolfe Island) and Hannah Breeze (? - 1836 Apr 28 Oneida County, NY)

   Died: 1928, buried at Cataraqui Cemetery

   Married: Fannie H. Tipson (? Ontario - 1878 January 28 Leeds, ON)

   Married: Barbara Crammand in 1878 (b. ? Scotland - 1908 May 26)

   1.1. William (1857 June 27 - 1910 May) m. Sarah Oram

   1.2. Frances Malvina (1860 - 1942 May 20) m. James Reid McFaul on 26 Nov. 1878; m. J. T. Ramsdell

   1.3. Matthew Robert (1861 Aug 15 - 1933 Jan 31 Kingston) m. Malissa Crammand

   1.4. George Andrew (1863 Battersea, ON - 1927 Dec 26 Frontenac) m. Martha Louise Barlow

   1.5. Ada Elizabeth (1865 Battersea, ON - 1900 25 May Kingston) m. Robert William Bryant

   1.6. Percilla (1867 - ?)

   1.7 Herbert (1870 June - 1871 Feb 5)

   1.8. John Howard (1872 NY - 1937 March 24)

   M. Jennie Shanessey

   1.8.1. Ruth (? - ?) m. A. I. Armstrong

   1.8.2. Lloyd John (1901 - ?) m. Jessie Annette Hutton (1898 - 1981 Nov 28 Toronto)

   1.8.2.1. Barbara (1926 - ?) m. Gordon Campbell

   1.8.3. Robert Melville (1904 - 1989) m. Donna Gordon (1905 - 1989)

   1.8.4. Dr. Colmer B.

   1.8.5. Carl Vaughn (1912 Sept 30 - 1976 June 3, funeral in Pickering, ON)

   M. Ada J. Armstrong (1911 - 1979 Apr 14 Abbotsford, BC)

   1.8.5.1. William Carl Irvine

   1.8.5.2. Shirley

   1.9. Hermand (1874 NY - 1885 Sept 25 Kingston)

The Gentile family

Crescenzo and Sylvia bought the Janetville mansion in December 1966, a little more than a year after Enzo bought the plastic housewares division of Rosedale Plastics International Ltd at 65 King Street in Lindsay and started Gentile Plastics.

Enzo Gentile was born in Italy. At age 16, he came to Canada and apprenticed as a tailor in Montreal on Rue Ste. Catherine. He made suits for businessmen, and though he tried to set-up a second store in the U.S., he found it not as profitable. The Americans didn't want to wear suits. A self-described rascal, he loved to dance with the "mademoiselles." He met Sylvia while he was in the U.S.; her family was involved in plastics manufacturing. Though they were polar opposites– Sylvia being a writer, singer, and more introverted– for Enzo, it was love at first sight. They married, Enzo left behind the tailor business, and ended up manager of Tucker Plastics in Coaticook, Quebec. In the 1980s, Tucker Plastics was known for their lawn decor, in particular, the bright pink plastic flamingos. Around 1966, Tucker Plastics sent a man to investigate the possible purchase of Rosedale Plastics in Lindsay. The word of the investigator was that the purchase wasn't worth it and the deal fell through. Though he had left Tucker Plastics and was selling encyclopaedias, Enzo heard about the fallen deal, and decided to pay a visit to the owner of Rosedale Plastics himself.

He travelled to London, England to meet with Mr. Rosenblum, where he was met with grand opulence. Enzo had no money in the bank. He went to England on a wing and a prayer with nothing but his dreams. He and Rosenblum got along well, and Enzo walked away with a deal to purchase Rosedale Plastics on a payment plan without any money down. The Gentile Plastics company was formed in partnership with his two brothers. They made items for household use like pails, laundry bins and dish racks, but in 1971, the Gentile brothers had a falling out and Enzo left the company.

Feeling the need to get away, to get some space between himself and his brothers, Enzo sold the Janetville mansion and, leaving behind his pregnant wife and their five children, he went to Venezuela, where he managed a plastics company, but soon found he didn't like the way the country conducted business, and he returned to Canada.

Sylvia and the children lived in Lindsay while Enzo was in South America. When he returned, he heard that Earl Jackson was in ill health and wanting to sell his restaurant. Enzo and Earl were friends, and though Enzo knew nothing about running a restaurant, he bought Jackson's Restaurant in November 1972. He brought Italian cuisine to Lindsay. He made his own noodles for ravioli and made the dough for pizza. He stressed that "in order to make good pizza, you must use good dough." When Jackson's opened under his management, Enzo gave away a free slice of pizza to all customers from 2 PM until closing. In October 1973, Enzo expanded operations and bought Graham's Bakery. The restaurant was a good place to sell the bakery items, and Enzo soon found he needed more restaurants for his baked goods, so he purchased a restaurant in Omemee and one in Peterborough.

During his time in Lindsay, Enzo championed for the town to rebuild the Old Mill at Kent Street East and repurpose it into a library and cultural centre. He faced a lot of opposition, mainly about the cost of such a project, but Enzo was so determined that he bought the old mill in January 1974, purchasing it from Russell Taylor and Gordon Henderson.

That same year, Enzo was a director for the Chamber of Commerce, and in the fall, he threw his hat into the elections for town council. He lost to Brenda O'Keefe. She won by 9 votes, but Enzo didn't want a recount. O'Keefe remembers Enzo came up to her and said, "I'm not going to ask for a recount, because I think that you'll do a good job." O'Keefe went on to serve on the Lindsay and Ops Planning Board, and the Lindsay Board of Parks Management. In addition to volunteering for Lindsay's museum, she also served on the Lindsay Public Library board and the Executive Committee for Community Improvements of the Downtown Business Area.

In the mid-70s, Enzo co-hosted a radio show with Don Sylvestre on CKLY called "Let's Discuss It," in which the hosts tackled local subjects that other media avoided in order to not "rock the boat." And rock the boat they did. On one particularly notable episode, the hosts discussed the perceived refusal of Lindsay Daily Post to publish a letter to the editor. The Post took exception to this. In their rebuttal editorial column published 22 April 1974, the editor said of the radio show, "Panel discussions by informed people concerning topics of interest to the community can be a good thing, but to permit two individuals to express their personal views on the air live, week in and week out, can become dangerous and damaging to the community especially when their thoughts become a mish-mash of personal views and misinformation." According

Enzo Gentile, seated in the front row at Monday night's council meeting, has some advice for council which he displays on a placard. Gentile wanted council to acquire the old mill on Kent St. East and renovate it for a library and the beginning of a cultural centre for Lindsay.   Post Staff Photo

Lindsay Post, 1972 November 29.

to The Post, the letter was received and sent to the publisher for approval, then to setting, where it was set in type and appeared in print as soon as possible. The writer contacted the editor about a spelling correction and was told the "correction would be made if the letter was approved for publication, the letter at the time being in the office of the publisher." The writer was not told if the letter would or would not be published. The Post finished its editorial by suggesting "the station management might be wise to check statements made by the commentators that could border on libel."

Lindsay Post, 1974.

In 1978, the old mill was destroyed by fire. In an interview with the Lindsay Post, Enzo praised God if the loss of the old mill meant town officials would take positive action to enforce the law and protect the citizens instead of protecting the criminals.

He did not have insurance on the building, and for this, he told reporters that he was glad "because people always are trying to accuse people of becoming rich at the expense of others. It would have had people think I had something to do with the fire to enrich myself." (Post 1978)

For years Enzo had tried to get the police to do something about the people breaking into the old mill. "Even though I had secured all accesses, youngsters were still finding their way in."

"If the burning of the old mill serves the purpose of opening the eyes of our town fathers and the administrators of the law to the widespread use of drugs and alcohol among our children so that positive steps will be taken to enforce the law and protect the citizens, then I praise God for what has happened."

Enzo Gentile

Years before, Enzo wrote an impassioned letter to the editor of the Post about the need for more education and legislation for alcohol and drugs. "More and more I have become exposed to people with drug or alcohol problems and every time I have asked them why, the answer has always been because of loneliness, not feeling wanted, too much pressure and related problems... Delinquent children are not born but raised by their parents and the environment in which they live." (Post 1974) For all his efforts, Enzo tried to improve the town, but received very little support.

Before the fire, Enzo had put the old mill up for sale, offering to include the architectural plans that he'd paid thousands of dollars to have drawn. The plans included a small restaurant, hotel and riverside cafe. Unfortunately, the mill did not sell.

The fire didn't merely destroy the old mill. It took everything from the Gentile family. The bank repossessed Graham's Bakery, the restaurants in Peterborough and Omemee, and their home. The family was forced to live in the basement of Jackson's Restaurant, as they had nowhere else to go. They showered at the Aquatorium (now the Lindsay Recreation Complex.) What few belongings they had left went into storage. The children slept in a store room, Sylvia slept on a cot in the office, and Enzo slept in the meat cooler.

While the community spewed accusations that Enzo had set the fire himself to collect the insurance money, the family suffered alone, without help from the community that Enzo had once championed. Enzo remembers crying one night in the basement of Jackson's Restaurant, at a loss for what to do, when he had a spiritual experience that told him his self-worth wasn't in the things he had, but within himself. Through this experience, he found the encouragement he needed to rebuild himself, his family and his business.

The Gentiles remained in Lindsay for two more decades. Jackson's Restaurant closed in 1982. From 1985 to 1991, Enzo worked for the Olympia Restaurant. Then, Enzo and Sylvia went to Israel, wanting to follow their connection with the Divine. They returned to Canada and now live with their son Matthew near Caledon, Ontario. Enzo has written about his life and his spiritual journey in a book titled, *On the Path to Glory*.

Their son Paul is an artist known for his miniature replica classical musical instruments. His renowned "Gentile Collection" of famous historic classical instruments included remarkably detailed, historically accurate miniatures of the 1679 Heller Stradivarius Violin; the Selmer Mark VI alto saxophone; the 1688 Antonio Stradivari Guitar; the 1701 Antonio Stradivari "Servais" Cello; the 1785 Vincenzo Panormo Double Bass; and the 1931 Eugene Sartori Double Bass Bow. He made a 1:7 replica of the 1903 Steinway White House Piano that was presented to President Theodore Roosevelt as a gift from the Steinway family to the people of the United States. The miniature doesn't just look exactly like the original, it's also fully functional. It is the only non-company instrument to ever earn the designation of Steinway & Sons piano.

Enzo's and Sylvia's granddaughter Julia is the successful musician, Vilivant, who began her recording career at age 14, when she was asked to record a song for the Pan Am Games. She recently completed a tour with the Matthew Goode band. Her vocal talents she gets from Sylvia, who was also a talented singer, and through her themes of 'moving forward,' 'self discovery' and 'purging' toxic elements from one's life, Enzo's fiery spirit lives on.

The Gordon family

LIVED IN THE HOUSE 1970 - 2021

The first time Jack Gordon heard about the Janetville mansion was when Enzo and Sylvia Gentile entered the Victoria Trust branch where Jack worked and applied for a mortgage.

The Gentiles showed Gordon a photo of the house. "I first saw an old photo of the house and was very impressed by the structure and size. I believe that old houses should be big and have a bay window, and a fireplace. We have four fireplaces here." (Kucherepa 1990)

When the Gentiles were ready to sell, Jack Gordon jumped on the chance to buy. Although he purchased the property in 1970, he didn't move in right away. Instead, he rented the house to the Kapitan family for two years.

In the hall on the second floor, Jack Gordon kept a green velvet lounge settee that Mark Kapitan remembers hiding behind as a child. When he returned to visit Jack in 2017, he was happily surprised to see the settee was still there.

In 1972, Jack Gordon let his twin sister, Jean and her husband, Douglas McInnes move in with their two daughters, Elizabeth and Lorraine. The family had been living in Waterloo. They occupied the house until 2008, when Doug's health declined and they needed to move to Lindsay.

The walls of the double parlour were painted Wedgwood blue to match the Wedgwood pottery collection.
    Gordon was an avid collector of antiques, adding many of the exceptional chandeliers that still grace the home. He travelled to England each year to buy antiques, often with an idea for what he was looking to add to his collection. One year he bought a French china cabinet, another year he bought an English clock.

Jack Gordon gave many tours of the house and grounds over the years, but none so well attended as the 2011 "Doors Open" tour. Doors Open is an annual event held across the province in which municipalities are encouraged to "open doors" of buildings that are normally closed to the public for educational purposes. Locations typically are chosen based on a theme and can include historic properties but also places like water treatment plants.

"It was a beautiful September day with nearly 400 people attending. The property was judged to be the most popular private residence in all of Ontario, receiving top award. A repeat tour took place again in 2014."

Jack Gordon, 2015.

Earl Grey

Earl Grey

Earl Grey

Passionfruit Fo

English Breakf

The Sopoci family

LIVED IN THE HOUSE 2021 - 2024

In 1978, Paulette Sopoci moved with her family from Pickering to a farm near Janetville. Her father, Paul, had a lifelong dream of owning a farm, a dream he'd carried since he was a child in the Slovak Republic and was finally able to fulfill in Kawartha Lakes when he purchased his own 200 acres. It was heavenly for Paulette to spend time riding horses with her sisters (she has a twin sister in a family of five girls) or to go to the barn to see the goats, pigs and cows or help during the haying season in the late fall. In a 2021 interview with Toronto Life magazine she said, "I lived an idyllic life as a farm girl. We may not have had trips to Disneyland, but if we wanted another pony, my dad would go to auction and buy one."

In Grade Two when she moved to Kawartha Lakes, Paulette now had to ride a bus to school. It was on these daily rides that she first saw the Janetville mansion. She remembers noticing the house and being in complete awe of it. It was the most stunning piece of architecture she'd ever seen. She didn't know anything more about the place, but she decided she was going to live there someday.

Her life took her to Toronto instead. After graduating highschool, she got a wonderful job for an entrepreneurial coaching firm and at twenty-four purchased her first loft. In 2004, she bought a four-bedroom house in Riverdale, overlooking Withrow Park. Within a year, she met her husband. They had two children, Jack and Avery. She thought this would be her forever home. She had worked her way up from receptionist for the coaching firm to one of the top of the salespeople on the team. In 2021 she was awarded Top International Sales Consultant of the Year by the International Association of Top Professionals. Her speaking engagements took her to the United Kingdom, Costa Rica, and South Africa.

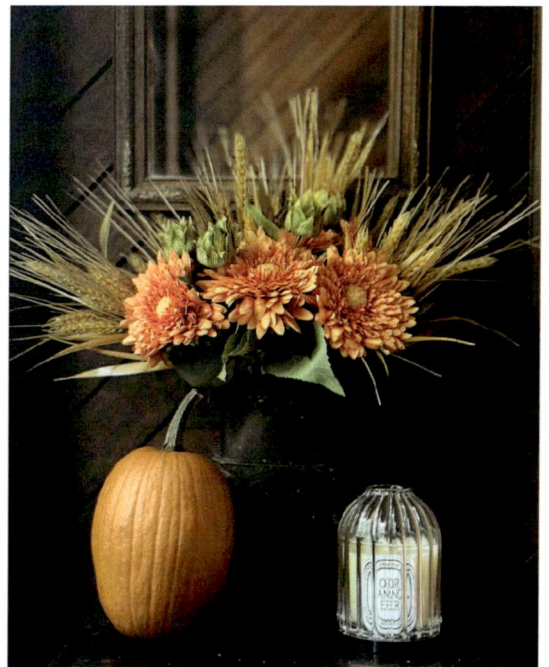

The pandemic hit. Paulette could no longer travel around the world as a professional speaker as she had for thirty years. She had to work from home. She and her husband separated. Her mother, Olga, was gravely ill in palliative care and passed away at the end summer in 2020. Her father had passed away ten years before.

In November, a friend mentioned to Paulette that the Janetville mansion was for sale. At the time, she was still grieving, and not considering moving or buying the house in Janetville, so she put the thought aside.

In January, Paulette found she was starting to feel disconnected from the career she'd built over thirty years, and when she sat down to do her yearly goal setting, she thought of the house again.

On a whim she checked to see if it was still for sale. It was. Without another thought, she decided she was going to buy the house. She didn't stop to consider how she would make it happen.

The next day, she drove to Janetville. She stood on the road, looking up at the grand Italianate mansion, and considered whether or not this was going to be the next chapter of her life. Was she certain? She came to the conclusion that she was.

Her friend warned her about the house's condition: "It's a dump." Paulette found the house had been left in disrepair for quite some time. There were bats living in the attic and the walls and ceilings were crumbling. But where others might see only the work required to fix the place, Paulette could see the beauty in the corbels, the grand archway between the parlours, the crown moldings. Everything about it was perfection, even though it needed a lot of work.

Throughout the renovation, Paulette wanted the house treated with huge respect. Honouring every element of the house that was historically protected was first and foremost. So much of the house was completely redone, but this also relieved the pressure of things going wrong or awry in the future.

Paulette truly believes this is the prettiest house in all of Ontario. She stands by this statement. "Imagine what that house would have looked like back in 1885, amongst the backdrop of humble farm homes and the beauty of the landscape of the backwoods of Ontario. It's such a hopeful place for the people in the neighbourhood, who would have no doubt appreciated having that doctor's house in Janetville." The grand archway in the double parlour. The moldings are 'extra' on so many levels. The high ceilings. The intricate inlaid pattern on the floors. There's nothing quite like it in any other house.

She named the house Primrose Hill Manor because she loves flowers and wanted to pay homage to the hillsides of the surrounding landscape. She didn't know anything about the home's history and was surprised to learn about Jane Primrose Nasmyth and Marjorie Primrose Nasmyth, who'd lived in the house long ago.

"I also love the fact that it was such a hopeful house back in the day, and I've always said that joy lives in that house. Yes, of course, life and death happened there, but it was and will, no doubt, be such a joyful place for the homeowners in the future."

In 2024, Paulette sold her beloved Primrose Hill Manor to move on to the next chapter of her life.

For the next homeowners, Paulette has this wish: "I just want any person who lives in that home, the next homeowners, and those that come after me many many years down the road, to just honour her beauty. Honour every little aspect of her, imperfections as well because all old homes come with it. She was so beautifully made that I just want the community to continue– the community and the world– to recognize the impact of this home for Kawartha Lakes and hopefully to bring joy to all that that drive by and see her grand presence along Janetville Road. I just want her to be taken care of. That's all. To be loved and to be appreciated and of course to see her in a movie or two, which I believe is going to be coming."

In the last weeks before she moved, Paulette posted the following on Instagram:

It's hard to process the overwhelming mix of emotions I am experiencing right now. How deeply our identities have been intertwined over the last three years. So before I make a post for my followers and your fans, my first letter is to you.

Dearest Primrose Hill Manor,
We found each other when we needed each other the most. You, in disrepair, desperately needing someone to give you life, and me recently divorced and stuck in pandemic limbo with a 30-year career that no longer challenged me. We needed each other, and most importantly, over time, we saved each other. And now, it's time to let each other go.
It will be ok because we are both stoic and strong. You have stood for 144 years and because of this small part I played, you will be here for many more decades to come. I am joyful and at peace.
You have made me realize what I am capable of. A single momma tackling your restoration, sharing your story with as many as I could, having a full time job, my real estate studies, my growing teens. Somehow I managed it all. And in you I found my strength.
In the coming weeks there will be many tears. But don't be surprised when I say these tears are not only of sadness but tears of joy and gratitude.
Joy, because I get to be part of your story forever, and gratitude because of the person you have made me become.

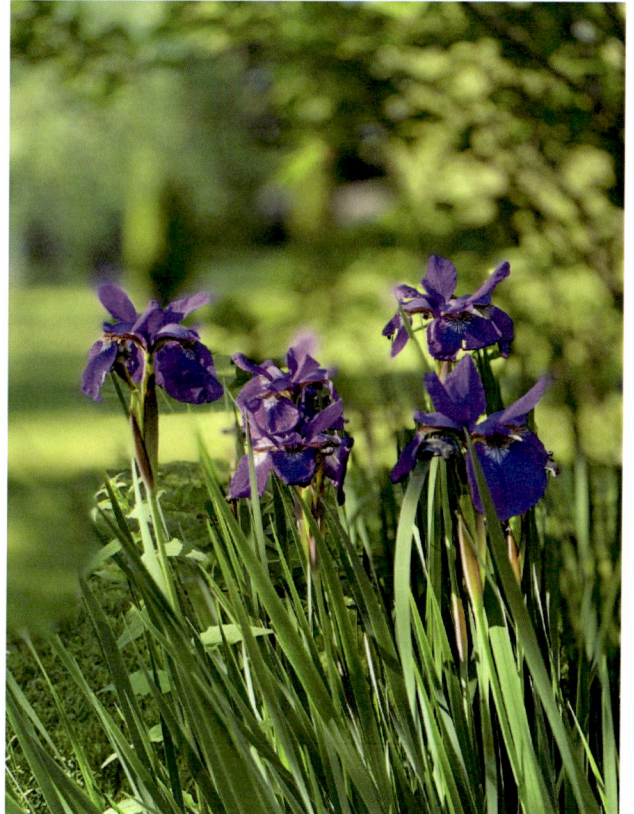

I had the time of my life! And now it's time to jump into the next chapter. New adventures await. Another oldie needs to be loved and just as importantly, it's time to be closer to family.

We are connected for life, sweet home and I will love you forever. I couldn't be more proud to be part of your story.

Paulette xo
May 6, 2021 to May 31, 2024

Sources

General Sources:

- Land registry

- Archive.org

- Ancestry.ca for birth, death, marriage, etc.

- FamilySearch.com for birth, death, marriage, etc.

- Findagrave.com

- Library & Archives Canada for First World War files

- Wikipedia

Train Information:

- http://www.trainweb.org/oldtimetrains/CPR_Trenton/History_Lindsay.htm

- https://railwaypages.com/lindsay-bobcaygeon-pontypool-railway

- *Narrow Gauge for Us: the story of the Toronto and Nipissing Railway.* Charles Cooper. Boston Mills Press. 1983.

- *Narrow Gauge Railways of Canada.* Omer Lavallée. Fitzhenry & Whiteside. 2005.

Early Landowners:

Lindsay Daily Post:
- 22 October 1952

First Doctor in Janetville:

Announcement of the College of Physicians and Surgeons of Ontario: for the academic year 1881-1882. Toronto. July 1881.

Announcement of the College of Physicians and Surgeons of Ontario: for the academic year 1885-1886. Toronto. June 1885.

The Union Publishing Co's Farmers' & Business Directory for the counties of Durham, Peterborough, Victoria. 1884.

Janetville Name Origin:

"Early Days in Manvers Recalled in Old Atlas; First Survey in 1816." *Thursday Post*. Lindsay. 1947 November 5.

Belden, H. *Illustrated Historical Atlas of the Counties of Northumberland and Durham, Ont.* 1878.

Library & Archives Canada. Post Offices and Postmasters collection.

"Minden." *Canadian Post*. Lindsay, Ontario. 19 August 1892.

"Nation's Most Unusual Store Once Prospered at Janetville." *Lindsay Post*. 22 October 1952.

"North Victoria Affairs." *The Watchman*. Lindsay, Ontario. 23 July 1891.

Architecture:

Blumenson, John. Ontario Architecture. Fitzhenry & Whiteside. Toronto. 1990.

Franck, Christine Huckins. "The Italianate Style in America." christinefranck.com

Humphreys, Barbara A. "The Architectural Heritage of the Rideau Canal." parkscanadahistory.com

Kyles, Shannon. www.OntarioArchitecture.com

Rodriguez, Jeremiah. "The yellow-paved history of Lambton County's butter brick buildings." The Sarnia Observer. August 2017.

"Rural Architecture: a two-story farm-house." The Canada Farmer. Vol. 2, no. 8. April 15, 1865. canadiana.ca

Sculptures:

www.galleriabazzanti.it/en/prodotto/marble-sculpture-bathing-venus/

The Lotus House:

Telephone conversation with Donald Sutcliffe. 2024 July 30.

Janetville History:

Carr, Violet. *The Rolling Hills*. Manvers Township Council. 1967.
   Curtis, Grant W. *The Women of Manvers: a brief biography and family recipes*. 2011.
   Hill, F.M. *The Statutes of the Province of Upper Canada (1792-1831): Together with Such British Statutes, Ordinances of Quebec, and Proclamations, as Relate to the Said Province by Ontario*. 1831.
   Leetooze, Sherrell Branton. The Trail through the Bush: a brief history of Manvers township. Lynn Michael-John Associates. Bowmanville, Ontario. 1998.

ALLAN FAMILY

Alphabetical list of graduates of the University of Edinburgh from 1859 to 1888 (both years included) with historical appendix (including present and past office bearers) and separate lists of honorary graduates and graduates with honours by University of Edinburgh. 1889.
The Canada Lancet, 1886.
The Benefactors of the University of Toronto, After the Great Fire of 14th February 1890. University of Toronto. 1892.

Historic Fogorig Farmhouse:

https://portal.historicenvironment.scot/designation/LB45774
https://canmore.org.uk/site/231203/fogorig
https://britishlistedbuildings.co.uk/200392790-fogorig-fogo/photos

Fogorig, Ontario:

Pierce, Lindi. "The Scottish Hearts of Fogorig." *County & Quinte Living magazine*. Metroland, Brighton, ON. Winter 2013.
https://www.fogorig.com
New York City Directory. R.L. Polk and co. 1917.

Newspapers:

Newspapers.com - following titles and editions:
   • San Francisco Call and Post, 21 October 1895

   • San Francisco Chronicle, 21 October 1895

   • San Bernardino Weekly Sun, 2 November 1895

   • San Francisco Call and Post, 23 April 1912

- San Francisco Call and Post, 28 December 1912

- New York Herald, 2 March 1922

- New York Times, 2 March 1922

- Los Angeles Times, 1 October 1923

- Hollywood Citizen News, 5 December 1939

- Visalia Times-Delta, 5 December 1953

Lindsay Daily Post - following editions:
- 11 October 1901

- 6 March 1903

- 3 July 1903

- 31 July 1903

- 4 December 1903

- 19 February 1904

- 30 December 1904

- 2 May 1905

- 9 May 1905

- 21 July 1905

- 22 December 1905

- 13 June 1906

- 18 June 1906

- 22 June 1906

- 26 November 1906

- 9 August 1907

- 22 October 1909

- 14 April 1910

- 19 February 1912

- 10 May 1918

- 15 August 1924

- 17 November 1924

Belleville Intelligencer, 5 August 1892.

Warder, Lindsay:
- 31 July 1885

- 10 August 1892

- 3 February 1893

- 7 August 1902

- 3 August 1905

- 10 August 1905

- 17 August 1905

- 19 June 1913

Powers, Sidney. *Oil and Gas in Oklahoma: petroleum geology in Oklahoma*. Norman. 1926.
Rutherfurd's southern counties register for ... being a supplement to the almanacs; containing accurate lists of the public bodies, registered electors, &c. and much useful information connected with the counties of Roxburgh, Berwick, Selkirk, & Peebles. 1858.
https://www.thewallstreetexperience.com/blog/uncovering-steamship-row-in-the-financial-district-of-nyc/
https://ephemeralnewyork.wordpress.com/tag/9-broadway-nyc/

NASMYTH FAMILY

https://airwar19141918.wordpress.com/tag/25-squadron-rfc/
https://matthewkbarrett.com/2015/05/22/the-veteran/#more-1531
The annual announcement of Trinity Medical School. Trinity Medical School. Toronto. 1887/1888.
De Ruvigny's Roll of Honour, 1914-1918, Volume 1. The Marquis De Ruvigny. Naval & Military Press. 2007.
The Canadian Medical Association Journal. Ed. by Andrew McPhail. Montreal. 1915.
Lacombe Guardian. Alberta. 2 June 1916.
Wright, Arthur Walker, editor. *Memories of Mount Forest and surrounding townships ... in honor of the Diamond Jubilee of the Confederation of the Dominion of Canada and of the founding of the Mount Forest Confederate, 1867-1927*. 1927.

Ketterson, Alexander. *On Active Service: a book of golden thoughts.* Hodder and Stroughton. New York. 1918.
Edwards, William J. *The Way We Were.* Boston Mills Press. 1979.
Skales, J.T. and G.F. Chapman. *Views of Mount Forest.* Mount Forest, Ontario. 1906.
"Political news: Grey South." *The Globe.* Toronto. 14 January 1875.

Newspapers:

Newspapers.com - following papers and editions:
- Baltimore Sun, 18 October 1899.
- Edmonton Journal. 19 January 1954.
- Evening Journal. Ottawa. 18 February 1889.
- Evening Review, East Liverpool, Ohio. 21 December 1920.
- Evening Review, East Liverpool, Ohio. 16 August 1932.
- Evening Review, East Liverpool, Ohio. 30 January 1933.
- Evening Review, East Liverpool, Ohio. 6 November 1954.
- Montreal Star, 1 November 1952.
- Mount Forest Representative. 14 August 1800.
- Red Deer Advocate. 21 April 1927.
- Sun. New York. 17 October 1899.
- World. New York. 17 October 1899.

Lindsay Post:
- 14 October 1898
- 24 July 1902
- 27 March 1905
- 29 April 1907
- 30 April 1907
- 12 July 1909
- 9 June 1916
- 10 November 1951

- 5 November 1952

- 5 November 1953

- 7 January 1954

Red Deer Advocate:
- 6 September 1928

- 13 September 1928

- 10 September 1941

Red Deer News:
- 19 July 1916

Watchman, Lindsay:
- 17 June 1897

- 7 February 1901

- 4 April 1907

MCCULLOCH FAMILY

Connor, Steve. "Flu epidemic traced to Great War transit camp." *The Independent*. 8 January 2000.

Newspapers:

Lindsay Post:
- 7 December 1906

- 17 January 1908

- 6 March 1908

- 10 July 1908

- 11 September 1909

- 21 October 1911

- 7 July 1916

- 5 February 1924
- 12 July 1924
- 13 August 1924
- 23 July 1925
- 23 September 1925
- 6 October 1926
- 7 October 1926
- 9 October 1926
- 12 September 1935
- 19 September 1945
- 8 April 1947
- 28 November 1973

JOHNSTON FAMILY

Newspapers:

Alexandria News:
- 9 May 1902
- 27 June 1902
- 29 August 1902
- 2 January 1903
- 1 January 1909
- 29 December 1911

Lindsay Post:
- 12 December 1908
- 30 April 1909

- 4 January 1910

- 2 January 1912

- 25 May 1917

Los Angeles Times:
- 1 September 1964

- 15 March 1990

Montreal Weekly Witness
- 27 February 1912

PORTER FAMILY

Newspapers:

Lindsay Post:
- 16 April 1920

- 18 March 1946

- 3 July 1957

- 17 July 1963

- 23 July 1964

- 29 July 1964

Quibell, Doris. Handwritten pages about family history and the Porter time in the house with four pages of genealogy. Sent to Paulette Sopoci. No date.

DAVIS FAMILY

Abbotsford News. 18 April 1979.

Arculus, Paul. *Steamboats on Scugog: a history of steamboating on the South Central Kawarthas*. Observer Publishing of Port Perry and The Port Perry Star Co. Limited. Port Perry, ON. 2000.

Armstrong, Alvin. *Buckskin to Broadloom: Kingston grows up*. Kingston Whig-Standard. Kingston. 1973.

Brashear, John A. *The Autobiography of a man who loved the stars*. Houghton Mifflin Company. New York. 1925.

Collins, Robert. *A Great Way to Go: the automobile in Canada*. Ryerson Press. Toronto. 1969.

Enright, Leo. "John A. Brashear and SL Phoebe: The Kingston Connection." *Journal of the Royal Astronomical Society of Canada*. April 2007.

Holthof, Benjamin L. *Kingston Inner Harbour: a cultural heritage landscape pilot study*. School of Urban and Regional Planning. Queen's University. Kingston. 2015.

Kingston Historical Society. *Historic Kingston: being the transactions of the Kingston Historical Society for 1953 - 54*. Kingston. 1954.

Newspapers:

Kingston British Whig:
- 26 April 1923

- 25 April 1928

Kingston Standard:
- 27 January 1937

- 25 March 1937

Kitchener-Waterloo Record:
- 2 December 1989.

Lindsay Post:
- 17 July 1963

- 3 March 1967

Toronto Star:
- 5 June 1976.

steamlaunch.wordpress.com: The Steam Launch Phoebe: Friends of the Phoebe supporting Kingston's history.

Turner, Larry, M.A. *Recreational Boating on the Rideau Waterway, 1890-1930*. Parks Canada. 1986.

GENTILE FAMILY

2024 June 9 - meeting with Enzo Gentile, his son Matthew Gentile, and Barbara Doyle at the Gentile home in Caledon, ON.

"Coaticook Town Council host to leaders of manufacturing plants." *Sherbrooke Daily Record*. 23 May 1961.

"L. Earle Wicklum." *National Post*. 15 March 1969.

Newspapers:

Lindsay Post:
- 19 October 1965

- 9 May 1967

- 18 November 1972

- 23 November 1972

- 29 November 1972

- 8 January 1973

- 4 October 1973

- 23 January 1974

- 30 January 1974

- 22 Apr 1974

- 24 Apr 1974

- 27 Apr 1974

- 30 Apr 1974

- 8 May 1974

- 3 July 1974

- 5 July 1974

- 21 October 1974

- 6 November 1974

- 12 November 1974

- 15 November 1974

"Lindsay's Old Mill: a treasure to be restored or a ruin to be demolished?" *Peterborough This Week*.
McKechnie, Ian. "The Life of Brenda O'Keefe." *Lindsay Advocate*. 22 October 2021.
O'Keefe, Brenda. "Brenda O'Keefe." Interviewed by Ian McKechnie for the Precious Memories Project. August 2019. Kawartha Lakes Museum & Archives.
Rogers, Alan. "Once tacky, now trendy, flamingoes flying high." *Ottawa Citizen*. 30 July 1985.

GORDON FAMILY

Kucherepa, Eugenie. "Historic Homes." *Lindsay Dimensions*. Volume 2, number 3. Lindsay, ON. Spring 1990.

Conversation with Mark Kapitan. April 4, 2024.

"Lot 6, Concession 13, Township of Manvers." Handwritten page of notes by Jack Gordon about history of property and recent upgrades. Found in box in attic by Paulette Sopoci. Dated July 23, 2015.

"Manvers Hall." Typed page of notes about the history of the property, focussed on the architecture, likely for the Doors Open tour of 2011. Found in box in attic by Paulette Sopoci. Hand dated June 11, 2014.

SOPOCI FAMILY

Kalinowski, Tess. "'I didn't have to be part of the rat race': COVID-19 helped these two Torontonians find a better life far from the big city." *Toronto.com*. 22 May 2021.

"Manifesting Dreams to Reality: Paulette Sopoci of Primrose Hill Manor." https://gossclub.com/paulette-sopoci/

"Paulette Sopoci selected as Top International Sales Consultant of the Year by IAOTP." https://www.prunderground.com/paulette-sopoci-selected-as-top-international-sales-consultant-of-the-year-by-iaotp/00218426/ 3 Feb 2021.

Rinaldi, Luc. "Growing up, she dreamed about owning this Kawartha Lakes mansion. She just bought it for $1.9 million." *Toronto Life* magazine. 20 May 2021.

Sopoci, Paulette. Instagram.

Sopoci, Paulette. Voice notes. Recorded June 2024.

Vyhnak, Carola. "'Magical castle' was her childhood dream home. Now she owns it." *Toronto Star*. 28 September 2022.

Photography Credits

Unless otherwise noted, all images are credited to Paulette Sopoci with the following exceptions:

Front cover and back cover: Jaime Espinoza, captivecamera.com

Page 1: Kim Magee Photography

Page 4, 6, 10, 11, 18, 22, 23,-24, 25-33, 42, 45, 56, 64, 75, 82: Jaime Espinoza, captivecamera.com

Page 8: Photo now with the Kawartha Lakes Museum & Archives

Page 49-50, 61: Sara Walker-Howe

Page 84: Edith Stewart. Courtesy Kawartha Lakes Museum & Archives

Page 122: unknown photographer, WaybackMachine.com

Page 123: unknown photographer. Courtesy Kawartha Lakes Museum & Archives

Chapter heading image made using Canva.com with art by Bokasana from bokasanavector.

Acknowledgements

There were so many interesting personal stories associated with Primrose Hill Manor, and I am eternally grateful with everyone for sharing their stories with me.

I would especially like to thank:

- Barbara Doyle at the Kawartha Lakes Museum & Archives for research assistance, image sourcing, road trips, and being an all-around cheerleader!

- Janet Cain for discussing early Janetville history and the village's early doctors with me.

- Mark Kapitan for the fascinating chat about your days living at the mansion and the history of masons.

- Donald Sutcliffe for chatting about your memories and family stories of Janetville and the mansion.

- Enzo and Matthew Gentile for meeting with me and Barbara to talk about your days in Janetville and Lindsay. Enzo, you are such a treasure!

- Emily Turner for reading the book in its messy stage and generously writing the Forward.

- Most of all, thank you to Paulette for choosing me to chronicle the mansion's history. It's been the gift of a lifetime!

Sincerely,
Sara

Milton Keynes UK
Ingram Content Group UK Ltd.
UKRC030830241024
2323UKWH00004B/19

* 9 7 8 1 0 6 8 8 4 5 4 1 3 *